D0962086

The

Gecko

An Owner's Guide To

A HAPPY HEALTHY PET

Howell Book House

Copyright © 1999 by Wiley Publishing, Inc., New York, NY

Howell Book House

Published by Wiley Publishing, Inc., New York, NY

All rights reserved. No part of this book may be reproduced or transmitted in any form or by any means, electronic or mechanical, including photocopying, recording, or by an information storage and retrieval system, without permission in writing from the Publisher.

No part of this publication may be reproduced, stored in a retrieval system or transmitted in any form or by any means, electronic, mechanical, photocopying, recording, scanning or otherwise, except as permitted under Sections 107 or 108 of the 1976 United States Copyright Act, without either the prior written permission of the Publisher, or authorization through payment of the appropriate per-copy fee to the Copyright Clearance Center, 222 Rosewood Drive, Danvers, MA 01923, (978) 750-8400, fax (978) 750-4744. Requests to the Publisher for permission should be addressed to the Legal Department, Wiley Publishing, Inc., 10475 Crosspoint Blvd., Indianapolis, IN 46256, (317) 572-3447, fax (317) 572-4447, E-Mail: permcoordinator@wiley.com.

Trademarks: Wiley, the Wiley Publishing logo and Howell Book House are trademarks or registered trademarks of Wiley Publishing, Inc., in the United States and other countries, and may not be used without written permission. All other trademarks are the property of their respective owners. Wiley Publishing, Inc., is not associated with any product or vendor mentioned in this book.

Limit of Liability/Disclaimer of Warranty: While the publisher and author have used their best efforts in preparing this book, they make no representations or warranties with respect to the accuracy or completeness of the contents of this book and specifically disclaim any implied warranties of merchantability or fitness for a particular purpose. No warranty may be created or extended by sales representatives or written sales materials. The advice and strategies contained herein may not be suitable for your situation. You should consult with a professional where appropriate. Neither the publisher nor author shall be liable for any loss of profit or any other commercial damages, including but not limited to special, incidental, consequential, or other damages.

For general information on our other products and services or to obtain technical support, please contact our Customer Care Department within the U.S. at 800-762-2974, outside the U.S. at 317-572-3993 or fax 317-572-4002.

Wiley also publishes its books in a variety of electronic formats. Some content that appears in print may not be available in electronic books.

Library of Congress Cataloging-in-Publication
Pavia, Audrey.
    The Gecko / Audrey Pavia
        p.   cm. — (An owner's guide to a happy healthy pet)
    Includes bibliographical references

    ISBN: 0-87605-212-X

    1. Geckos as Pets.   I. Title.   II. Series.
SF459.G35P29   1998
639.3'95—dc21

98-35546
CIP

Manufactured in the United States of America
10 9 8 7 6 5 4 3

Series Director: Amanda Pisani
Series Assistant Director: Jennifer Liberts
Book Design: Michele Laseau
Cover Design: Iris Jeromnimon
Illustration: Steve Adams
Photography:
   Front cover by Bill Love; Inset photo by L. Puente; Back cover by Bill Love
   Joan Balzarini: 26
   Zig Lesczcynski: 7, 8, 11, 13, 22, 23, 32, 34, 38, 41, 45, 46, 48, 50, 54, 55, 58, 60, 62, 66, 67, 70, 73, 74, 76, 78, 83, 86, 89, 90, 93, 95, 99, 100, 102, 106, 108, 111, 118
   W. B. Love: i, 2–3, 5, 9, 16, 17, 25, 29, 33, 59, 64–65, 105, 109
   Aaron Norman: 18, 20–21, 61, 81
   L. Puente: 112, 119
   David Schilling: 51
   Judith Strom: 37
   John Tyson: 43
   B. Everett Webb: 35, 114, 122
Production Team: Carrie Allen, Ellen Considine, Kristi Hart, Clint Lahnen, Dennis Sheehan, Terri Sheehan

Contents

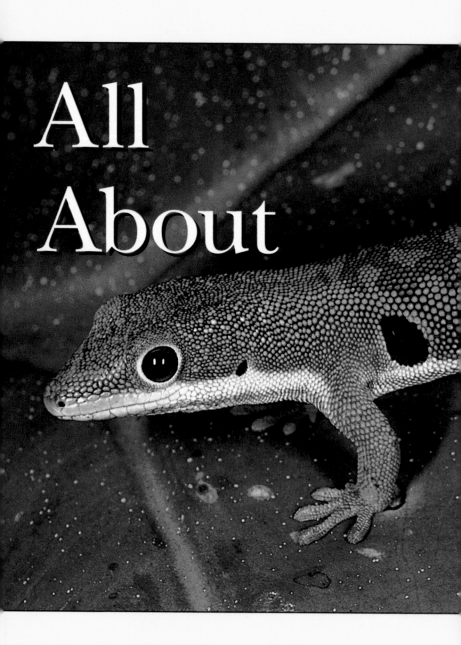

All About

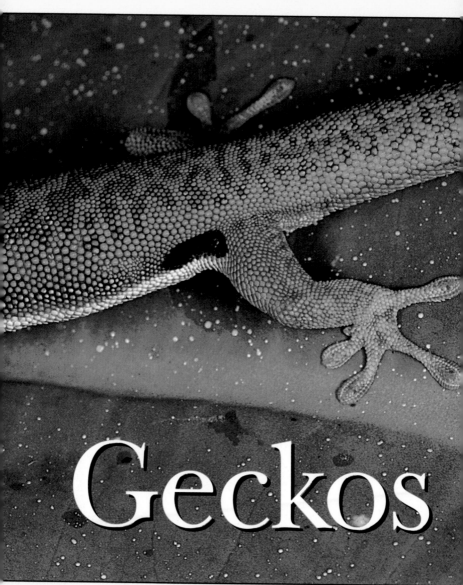

part one

Geckos

External Features of the Gecko

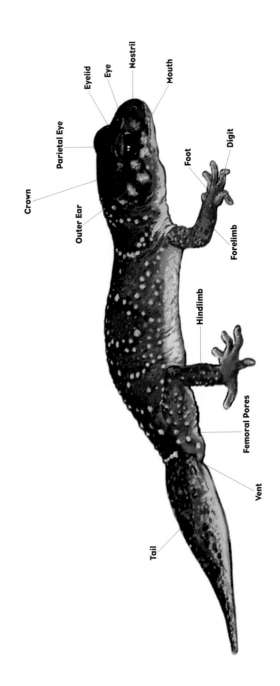

Parietal Eye

Eyelid

Eye

Nostril

Mouth

Crown

Outer Ear

Foot

Digit

Forelimb

Hindlimb

Femoral Pores

Vent

Tail

chapter 1

What Is a Gecko?

You've seen a gecko somewhere, or maybe you already own one. That's why you are reading this book. There is something very special about geckos, something that draws us to them. Is it their wondrous colors and interesting patterns? Or could it be their unusual shape that sets them apart from other lizards? How about their calm and somewhat comical nature? Do we relate to it in some way? There is also a mystique inherent to geckos, and this is undoubtedly one of the things that fascinates us about them. As we watch them go about their daily lives, we can only wonder what goes on in

their minds. Anyone who has observed a gecko for a period of time knows that there is a lot more to these intriguing animals than meets the eye.

Whatever our reasons for fascination with the gecko, there is one thing for certain: Living with one of these beautiful creatures enhances our lives and brings us closer to nature. While geckos won't interact with us like our pet dogs and cats do, they can still provide companionship in their own quiet and subtle way.

A Member of the Lizard Family

Geckos are part of the reptile class of vertebrates (animals with spines), and they have a number of things in common with their reptile cousins, namely snakes, turtles and other lizards. Like other reptiles, geckos have dry scales on their bodies. These scales are replaced regularly through the process of shedding, technically called *ecdysis*. Reptiles have very few—and in some cases no—glands in their skin.

The internal organs of reptiles are similar to those of humans and other mammals. For example, reptiles have a heart, lungs and a digestive system that aren't very different from our own.

Geckos belong to the lizard group, which is the largest group within the reptile class. There are nearly 5,000 different species of lizards in the world, living in the parts of the globe that are the warmest.

Lizards possess certain traits that set them apart from other reptiles. Most lizards have arms and legs, tails and body scales. Most lizard species also have eyelids (unlike snakes, which have none). Don't be misled, though: There are many geckos that are exceptions to this rule.

Geckos rank among some of the smallest lizards in the world. The *Lipidoblepharis sanctaemartae* gecko measures in at only around 1½ inches long. The biggest gecko is *Rhacodactyulus leachianus,* which grows to a total of 14½ inches long. By comparison, the largest modern lizard ever discovered is the Komodo Monitor

(Varanus komodoensis), which can grow to be longer than 10 feet.

All Kinds of Geckos

There are around 700 different species of geckos in the world, each of which falls under one of four sub-families within the larger *Gekkonidae* family: *Eublepharinae*, *Diplodactylinae*, *Gekkoninae* and *Sphaerodactylinae*. Only a handful of these many species are traditionally kept in captivity.

Geckos are found in great abundance throughout the world. In fact, only four species are considered as en-dangered or threatened. The *Phelsuma guentheri*, *Sphaerodactylus micropithecus*, *Cyrtodactylus serpensinsula* and *Phelsuma edwardnewtoni* geckos make up this short list and should never be sold as pets or captured.

Like other lizards, geckos produce eggs and have scales that they regularly shed. (Madagascar Giant Day Gecko)

In the United States, there are five native species, and about fif-teen species that have been introduced to the U. S. environment. All of these geckos live in the southern portion of the country and can be found in California, Nevada, Arizona, New Mexico, Texas, Louisi-ana, Alabama, Georgia, Mississippi and Florida.

Geckos live in a variety of habitats. While all liz-ards dwell in the warmer areas of the world, gec-kos in particular live in temperate, tropical and sub-tropical climates. Geckos survive in both very humid environments and very dry ones. They make their homes in the rain forest, on high plateaus, in sandy deserts and even in human dwellings.

Gecko Details

You've probably noticed that geckos look somewhat different from other lizards. This is because they have several distinctive traits.

Geckos have triangular-shaped heads and distinct necks. (African Fat-tailed Geckos)

HEAD

One of the easiest traits to spot is the construction of their head. Geckos tend to have a triangular-shaped head, while most other lizards have a more stream-lined, V-shaped head. The other lizards' heads seem to flow right into their body. Geckos, however, usually have a discernible neck that attaches their unusual head to their body.

Some geckos have adhesive pads on their feet to help climb almost any suface. (Tokay Gecko)

FEET

The feet of many geckos have adhesive pads on their bottoms that allow the gecko to stick to just about any surface. Not all geckos have these pads, but the ones that do can hold on pretty tight when they want to— even when they are upside down.

TAIL

One of the gecko's most distinctive characteristics is its tail. Rather than being long and narrow as on other lizards, a gecko's tail is usually narrow at the base, thick in the middle and narrow at the tip. Unlike other lizards, many geckos use their tails to store fat for those times when food might be scarce. But just like other lizards, geckos are *autotomous*. That means they can detach their tails to distract predators. The detached tail will wiggle and writhe, keeping the predator from noticing that the best part of the meal is getting away.

The gecko's autotomous nature is one reason why it's so important to handle geckos carefully: Their tails are easily detached when they are roughly handled, even by well-meaning humans.

VOICE

Many gecko species are able to vocalize. Of those that can, the male gecko uses its voice to warn away intruders to its territory and also to attract a mate; the female can also produce sounds. This makes geckos a somewhat unique family in the lizard world because most other lizards are relatively silent.

In the daylight, nocturnal geckos' pupils appear to be vertical slits; at night their pupils dilate to encompass nearly the entire eye. (Uroplatus lineatus)

EYES

The eyes of the gecko vary depending on the species. Most geckos are nocturnal (active mostly at night) and so have pupils that look like vertical slits when viewed in the daylight. These nocturnal geckos have very strong night vision, and their pupils will dilate to encompass nearly the entire eye. A few geckos are diurnal, meaning that they are most active during the day. These geckos have round pupils that look somewhat like ours.

The majority of gecko species don't have eyelids, which makes them similar to most other reptiles. However, some species of geckos—such as the Leopard Gecko—do have eyelids.

All geckos actually lick their eyeballs with their tongue. While scientists aren't completely sure why they do this, many suspect this is the gecko's way of keeping the eye area clean.

EARS

Gecko ears are another fascinating part of the lizard's anatomy. If you hold certain gecko species up to the light, you can actually see through their ear canals out to the other side! But don't let that fool you into thinking that there is not much in there. The gecko ear is complicated, and geckos can hear better than most other lizards. Geckos need good hearing to be able to effectively communicate with members of their own species. It's also possible that they use their hearing when hunting for prey.

ENDOLYMPHATIC SACS

Some species of geckos in the *Gekkoninae* genus have large sacs on either side of their necks. These sacs are actually reservoirs for calcium. Scientists aren't sure why some geckos have these bulging sacs, but they surmise it could be to help female geckos form egg shells, or to help in the metabolism of calcium.

REPTILE SENSES

Although lizards and snakes are classified together in the superorder Squamata, their sensory abilities are quite different. Lizards, including geckos, have a well-developed sense of taste. Along with the ability to taste with their tongues, most lizards have what is known as a Jacobson's organ in their mouths. This feature, which they share with snakes, enables them to sense chemical traces in the environment. It almost provides them with a "sixth sense." Snakes rely very heavily on the information received through their Jacobson's organ, in large part because they have quite poor vision. They need the "extra sensors" to locate food. Lizards, in contrast, have good vision, and a strong sense of taste in their tongues. They also have the ability to hear quite well; whereas snakes are essentially deaf.

DIET

One characteristic that all geckos share is a penchant
for eating bugs. Without exception, all gecko species
are insectivores, but some will eat other foods as well.
Tokay Geckos, for example, have been known to drink
nectar as an occasional treat. Larger species will also
eat small mammals, such as newborn mice.

Other Reptilian Traits

Despite all their differences, there are many traits that
geckos have in common with their reptilian cousins.

BODY TEMPERATURE

Geckos, like all reptiles, are ectothermic, which means
that they are unable to internally regulate their own
body temperatures the way that mammals can. Instead,
geckos rely on outside sources to stay warm or cool,
and must move from place to place to keep their body
temperatures just right. In the early morning, a gecko
will seek a warm sunlit place to heat up its body. Once
the sun becomes too hot, however, the gecko will move
to a shady area so its body temperature can cool down.

*Geckos use their
long, broad
tongues to "taste"
or determine the
nature of things
in their environ-
ment. (Four Spot
or Peacock
Madagascan Day
Gecko)*

TASTE AND SMELL

Like other lizards, geckos use their tongues to "taste"
things in their environment. Their long, broad
tongues reach out to pick up molecules in the air.

These molecules are brought back into the mouth where they come into contact with the Jacobson's organ, located in the palate. This organ enables the gecko to determine the exact nature of whatever it is the gecko has tasted—whether it be an unrecognized insect, an obstacle in its path or your hand.

SKIN

Geckos and other lizards have an outer layer of skin made up of keratin. This layer is shed in patches as the gecko grows. They also have an inner layer of skin that contains a large number of blood vessels. Both layers of skin are very delicate and tear easily.

Scientific Names

When learning about geckos, it is helpful to understand the ways that scientists have named the different species. Common names like Banded Gecko and Day Gecko are not always used by reptile hobbyists and writers. You'll find that in many cases, your favorite gecko species is identified by its scientific, Latin name. For example, the popular Leopard Gecko is known by scientists as *Eublepharis macularius*. When you go into a pet store where species are labeled by their scientific names in their display cages, or try to look up information on the Leopard Gecko in the library, knowing the species' scientific name will be a great help to you.

There's another good reason to know a gecko's scientific name: Common gecko names, like Wall Gecko and Frog-Eyed Gecko, for example, are not always used in the same way. Some hobbyists may refer to a gecko by one common name, while others use a different moniker. The only way to know for certain which gecko is being discussed is to look at the species' scientific name.

If you develop a basic understanding of how scientific names are developed and used, you'll be able to understand a lot about different gecko species just by seeing the gecko's official name.

Within the four subfamilies of geckos—*Eublepharinae, Diplodactylinae, Gekkoninae* and *Sphaerodactylinae*—there are a number of genera. And within each of these genera are individual species. Some species are further divided into subspecies.

The four subfamilies of geckos represent species with qualities that are unique to each. By knowing which subfamily a gecko belongs to, you will automatically know certain things about that species. Because the subfamily names are not included in the scientific name of the species—as you will see it when you are doing research or looking at specimens at zoos and pet stores—it's helpful to know which genera fit into which subfamilies.

The Blue-tailed Day Gecko is also known as Phelsuma cepediana, *a member of the* Gekkoninae *subfamily.*

Eublepharinae

Geckos in the *Eublepharinae* subfamily are distinguished from the other subfamilies by several features. Each species has moveable eyelids, no adhesive toe pads and typically lays up to two soft-shelled eggs at a time. There are five gecko genera in the *Eublepharinae* subfamily: *Aeluroscalabotes, Coleonyx, Eublepharis, Hemithecus nyx* and *Holodactylus.*

Typical *Eublepharinae* subfamily geckos are the Leopard Gecko, African Fat-Tailed Gecko and the Banded Gecko.

Diplodactylinae

The genera in the *Diplodactylinae* subfamily include *Carphodactylus, Crenadactylus, Diplodactylus, Eurydactylodes, Heteropholis, Heteronotia, Hoplodactylus, Lucasium, Naultinus, Nephrurus, Oedura, Phyllurus, Pseudothecadactylus, Rhacodactylus, Rhynchoedura,* and *Underwoodisaurus.* Two species in this subfamily are the Robust Velvet Gecko and Thick-Tailed Gecko.

The *Diplodactylinae* subfamily features geckos with no eyelids and that lay two soft-shelled eggs. Some of these lizards have adhesive toe pads, while others do not.

Gekkoninae

The *Gekkoninae* subfamily features by far the largest number of gecko genera—a whopping sixty-four. Geckos in this subfamily have no eyelids, usually lay two hard-shelled eggs and some species have sticky toe pads.

The genera in this subfamily are: *Afroedura, Agamura, Ailuronyx, Alsophylax, Ancylodactylus, Aristelliger, Bavayia, Blaesodactylus, Bogertia, Briba, Bunopus, Calodactylus, Chondrodactylus, Cnemaspis, Colopus, Cosymbotus, Crossobamon, Cyrtodactylus, Dravidogecko, Ebenavia, Garthia, Geckolepis, Geckonia, Gehyra, Gekko, Gymnodactylus, Hemidactylus, Hemiphyllodactylus, Homonota, Homopholis, Kaokogecko, Lepidodactylus, Luperosaurus, Lygodactylus, Millotisaurus, Narudasia, Pachydactylus, Palmatogecko, Paragehyra, Perochirus, Phelsuma, Phyllodactylus, Phyllopezus, Pristurus, Pseudoceramodactylus, Pseudogekko, Ptenopus, Ptychozoon, Ptyodactylus, Quedenfeldtia, Rhacodactylus, Rhoptropella, Rhotropus, Saurodactylus, Stenodactylus, Tarentola, Teratolepis, Teratoscincus, Thecadactylus, Trachydactylus, Trigonodactylus, Tropiocolotes, Uroplatus,* and *Wallsaurus.*

Three common geckos in the *Gekkoninae* subfamily are the Helmeted Gecko, the Tokay Gecko and the Day Gecko.

Sphaerodactylinae

The *Sphaerodactylinae* subfamily of geckos contains species with no eyelids and that typically lay only one hard or soft-shelled egg. The subfamily features the *Coleodactylus, Gonatodes, Lepidoblepharis, Pseudogonatodes* and *Sphaerodactylus* genera. The Reef Gecko and White-Throated Gecko are two examples from this subfamily.

WHAT'S IN A NAME

In most situations you will encounter, the subfamily name is not provided as part of the scientific name, nor is the subspecies name. The genus and species names are most commonly used. So, if you are standing in a pet store looking at a gecko labeled *Hemitheconyx caudicinctus,* you'll know that you are looking at a member of the genus *Hemitheconyx* (the genus always starts with a capital letter), and the species *caudicinctus.* In most cases, the scientific name will appear in italic print, as it does in this book.

If you have a good memory and you want to become a gecko expert, you will start to memorize these scientific names and put them together with their common names. It won't be long before you know that the *Hemitheconyx caudicinctus* you are looking at in the pet store is more commonly called the African Fat-Tailed Gecko. You will also be able to ascertain, just by seeing its scientific name and knowing which subfamily its genus belongs to (*Eublepharinae*), that this gecko has moveable eyelids, no adhesive toe pads and lays two soft-shelled eggs at a time.

chapter 2

The History of Geckos

The natural history of the gecko is fascinating, and it takes us back to nearly the very beginning of life itself. The direct ancestor of today's gecko is the early reptile, which appeared nearly 300 million years ago, according to fossil records. Since that time, nearly all the life we see on Earth today evolved from these first reptiles—including ourselves.

When the ancestors of our pet geckos first began to walk the Earth, the planet was very different than it is now. The geologic time period known as the Carboniferous Period, which occurred within the Paleozoic Era, represents a still relatively young Earth with a warm, moist climate. Giant plants reached up toward the sun, and huge insects filled the air. It was in this environment that the first reptiles evolved from amphibians, creatures that had crawled from the sea.

The Age of the Reptile

The very first reptiles that have been identified as such were creatures called Cotylosaurs. These ancestors of the gecko and other lizards measured around 3⅓ feet long and had short necks, stubby legs and very long tails.

A million or so years later, the Earth began to cool somewhat, and the Permian Period began. The continents began to develop, the atmosphere and the oceans began to cool, and the air became somewhat drier. The insects got smaller and reptiles began to prosper. (It's interesting to note that reptiles have been feeding on insects since the Carboniferous Period, something all geckos still do today.)

Ancestors of today's geckos became prevalent in the Mesozoic Era. (Japanese Leopard Gecko)

It wasn't until the Mesozoic Era, also known as the Age of Reptiles, that the ancestors of today's geckos became prevalent all over the Earth. Dinosaurs began evolving from early reptiles during the Triassic Period of the Mesozoic Era, as did the first early mammals. A few million years later, during the Jurassic Period, these dinosaurs came to dominate the land, oceans and air. Dinosaurs in various shapes and sizes inhabited nearly the entire planet. Eventually, birds evolved during this period as well.

Sometime during the Cretaceous Period, around 65 million years ago, the dinosaurs somehow became extinct. There are many theories on how this occurred, but one thing is for certain: Whatever wiped out the dinosaurs did not kill all the reptiles on Earth. In fact, not long after the extinction of the dinosaurs, other large reptiles continued to roam the planet. The giant Mosasaur was one of these survivors. It lived in the

ocean and swam using its short paddles and long tail.
In the air, Pterosaurs, a flying lizard, still survived.

The gecko of today is the evolutionary descendent of
those reptiles that survived beyond the dinosaurs.
Geckos have a lot in common with their prehistoric
an-cestors, and little has changed in their biology over
the eons. In fact, geckos are among the most primi-
tive lizards alive today. We can appreciate our pet
geckos as not only links to nature, but links to the very
distant past.

Humans and Geckos

No one knows exactly when human beings began keeping lizards as pets, but we can surmise that the practice
started a long time ago. It is clear through both art and
scientific literature that our species has been fasci-
nated by lizards for thousands of years.

*People have been
charmed by geckos
for many years;
some, such as the
Tokay Gecko, are
considered good
luck.*

Geckos have lived in close association with humans for
a long time. Geckos in various parts of the world can
be found co-habitating with humans in their dwellings. These are not "pet" geckos per se, but rather wild
lizards that have wandered into human homes in
pursuit of insects. Because geckos are so good at eating bugs, they are welcome in most homes. In fact, in
Malaysia having a Tokay Gecko in your home is considered good luck.

In the southwestern United States, geckos lived closely with Native Americans in the desert environment. These geckos, which were probably ancestors of the Banded Geckos we see today, were often the subject of Native American art. Their images have survived in the form of rock art, pottery, jewelry and fetishes. The stylized representation of a gecko shown on so much Native American art has even come to represent the spirit of the Southwest.

Human admiration for the gecko eventually culminated in North America in the late twentieth century. People in both the United States and Canada began developing a strong interest in keeping these fascinating lizards as pets. While in the 1960s and 1970s geckos were only rarely seen in pet stores, a small lizard called the Anole was commonly sold as a pet. These hardy little lizards were sold as pets for children. There was also a trend in the 1950s for women to "wear" Anoles on their clothing. The lizard would be attached to a pin with a small leash.

In the last decade there has been a huge increase in the popularity of lizards as pets (not as pins) with both children and adults. Consequently, there are now a number of lizard species available to the average reptile fan.

Because many gecko species are easy to breed in captivity and even easier to keep, the gecko in particular has grown in popularity. Nearly every pet store in the United States that sells lizards carries geckos. The Leopard Gecko is the most popular gecko pet and is readily available to any lizard keeper.

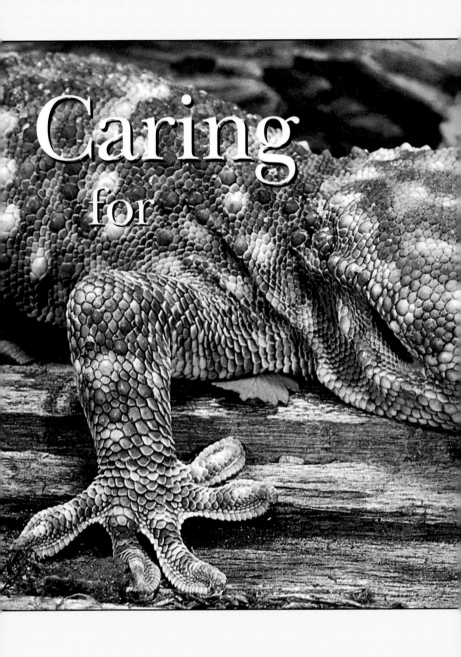

Caring
for

part two

Your

Gecko

chapter 3

Choosing Your Gecko

Geckos are beautiful and amazing creatures, and many humans are drawn to them. But before you run out and buy one of these animals, there are a few care and keeping issues you need to take into consideration.

Responsibilities of Gecko Ownership

Compared to a dog or cat, a gecko is a fairly easy pet to own. The owner of a gecko can leave his or her pet alone for several hours a day or even for days without having to worry about the need for bathroom breaks. There's no need to go to a veterinarian once a year for preventative care, such as examinations and inoculations, and there's no hair to wipe off your couch before company comes over.

22

On the other hand, geckos are not entirely maintenance-free pets. Some species are very demanding and need a lot of specialized care. Even geckos that are easy to keep need to (at least) have their water changed daily. You can't just ignore a gecko for days at a time. If you do, your pet won't be around for very long.

WILL YOU HAVE TIME TO CARE FOR A GECKO?

To determine whether or not gecko ownership is right for you, think about your lifestyle. Will your job, school or other commitments allow you to set aside time every day to care for your gecko? With even the easiest species to keep, your pet will need to have its water changed, its enclosure cleaned of waste and dead insects, and the temperature checked every day. Every

Each species demands its own level of care, but all geckos need some daily attention. (Barbour's Day Gecko)

other day or so, your gecko will also need to be fed. If you are providing your pet with commercially bred insects, you will have to make a trip to the pet supply store every two weeks to purchase the insects and will have to care for the insects from the time you buy them to the time your pet consumes them. If your lizard is also to eat wild-caught insects (that have not been sprayed by insecticides), you will have to find time to go outside and collect them.

Moreover, if you have chosen one of the more demanding species of gecko, you will have to make time to spray its terrarium with water one or more times a day. You will also need to carefully monitor the temperature and humidity in its enclosure.

And don't forget vacations. Some gecko species can go a few days without much in the way of attention as long as they have food, water and a reliable heat source. But the more demanding species will need to be checked on more than once a day.

Take all of this into consideration when you are making the decision about whether to add a gecko to your household. If you have some time to care for a reptile pet, but not a significant amount, consider purchasing one of the species that is easier to care for. These geckos are not only less work, but they are more likely to survive to a ripe old age.

You should also consider whether your home can accommodate a gecko's housing. Depending on the species you choose and the number of lizards you intend to keep, do you have enough room in your home for the appropriate-sized terrarium? Don't short-change your gecko because you want to economize space. Geckos are happiest in roomy enclosures, and it is unkind to deprive them of the space they need.

JOIN YOUR LOCAL HERPETOLOGICAL SOCIETY

Enhance the educational value of your pet lizard by joining a local herpetological society. These groups will conduct seminars and provide literature on all aspects of lizard care. Other experienced lizard owners can share their tips with you. Best of all, many societies work to ensure the safety of lizards in their natural environment. By getting involved, you can learn about lizards and help to protect them at the same time.

You may like the way geckos look and that's why you are attracted to them. But if you want a lizard that you can handle on a regular basis, you might want to consider another kind of pet. Geckos are primarily considered display lizards and should not be subjected to constant handling.

GECKOS AND KIDS

If you are buying a gecko for your children, think very carefully before you make your purchase. Consider whether your kids are old enough to learn to respect the gecko and admire it only from afar. Geckos should not be handled by young children. A gecko's delicate skin is easily damaged, and a fall can kill or seriously injure a gecko. A lost tail, something that can occur with rough handling, can jeopardize a gecko's health in certain situations.

Very young children cannot be expected to understand that a gecko should not be touched. If you can't find a way to keep the gecko out of the reach of a small child, you should consider waiting until your child is older. If you already have older children, will you still take on responsibility for the gecko's care, despite their promises that they will care for the pet themselves? Even though they have the best of intentions, most children do not have the attention span required for the care of a gecko or any pet.

Geckos are best kept as display lizards—they are not rough-and-tumble pets for children. (Phelsuma quadriocellata lepida)

If you decide to give your child partial responsibility in caring for the gecko, you should always be there to monitor the pet's well-being. No child should be given unsupervised responsibility for any animal. Children cannot be expected to recognize signs of illness. An adult should always be a pet's primary caregiver. Any other arrangement could result in harm to the gecko, either through neglect or inexperience on the part of the child. And, when the child eventually loses interest in the pet, as most do, it will be your responsibility to take over completely.

GECKOS AND OTHER PETS

If you have other pets, such as a cat or dog, you also need to think about keeping your gecko safe from them. Cats and dogs should not be allowed unsupervised access to your gecko's enclosure. A cat or dog with strong predatory instincts can make short work of a gecko. Even if your cat or dog doesn't outwardly harm the gecko, constant harassment can result in a fatal dose of stress for your lizard.

COST CONSIDERATIONS

Another consideration when thinking about gecko ownership is cost. The price of the gecko and its cage will be your primary financial commitment, but these items can cost you hundreds of dollars, depending on the type of species you choose and the number of geckos you want to own. Once your pet is set up in its new home, the amount of money you will have to spend on food for your pet will be negligible. However, should your gecko become ill, it is your responsibility to take it to a veterinarian. Depending on what is wrong with your pet, this may cost you a good amount of money.

Responsible gecko ownership includes caring for its health needs, including veterinary visits when necessary. (African Fat-Tailed Gecko)

But most important of all, are you willing to make an emotional commitment to your gecko? Are you prepared to accept responsibility for a living creature that is solely dependent on you for its well-being? Are you willing to make your pet's health and safety a priority in your life? If your answer to these questions is yes, then you just may be ready to join the ranks of gecko owners everywhere.

Where to Get Your Gecko

Do not purchase a gecko impulsively. All pets need and deserve a certain level of commitment from their owners. Some geckos can live as long as twenty years. The attractive little gecko in the window may be tiny now, but in six months to a year, it may be eight inches or larger, depending on the species. Whatever its size, the lizard will require daily care. Impulse purchases of pets often result in unhappiness for the owner and a sorry fate for the pet.

In most situations, you will have to actually purchase your gecko. There are exceptions to this: You may know someone who wants to give away a gecko because they can no longer take care of it. Your local reptile veterinarian may have a gecko that was abandoned by its owner and needs a new home. On occasion, your local animal shelter may have a gecko available for adoption, or you may know of a reptile rescue group in your area that is trying to find a home for a gecko. These situations are relatively rare.

BREEDERS

One good place to buy a gecko is from a responsible breeder. These are gecko experts who keep their animals in clean and healthy environments. They are authorities on their species of choice. Because some species do not breed readily in captivity, it may be hard to find them. However, some of the more popular species, which are best suited to novice gecko owners, can be purchased from breeders fairly easily.

SPECIALTY STORES

Another fine source for purchasing a gecko is a retail pet store that specializes in reptiles. These reptile stores usually purchase their animals directly from breeders and wholesalers, and employees are often adept at caring for the lizards until they go into permanent homes. The geckos that have been imported and are to be sold through these shops have usually been acclimated and therefore tend to be healthy.

Buying your pet from a responsible breeder or reptile store will help to ensure that you are obtaining the species of gecko that is best for you. There are many different gecko species, each with its own special qualities and needs. A breeder or reptile store employee can talk to you about the level of care for the species in which you are interested and help you determine whether or not you have the time and experience to take on the job.

Most gecko breeders are located in Florida and California. If a reputable breeder is within driving distance to you, you may want to go there in person to select your gecko. Be aware that a responsible breeder will welcome you, as a prospective buyer, into his or her breeding facility, allowing you to see first-hand the environment in which the gecko has been living. This way, you will be able to gauge whether or not your prospective pet has been well cared for and is living in clean and healthy conditions.

Buying from a breeder also offers an added bonus. Once you purchase your gecko, you go home with the name and phone number of an experienced contact who can answer your questions and provide you with help should you need it.

While being able to visit the breeder in person is the best scenario, in most cases buying from a breeder means buying your pet sight unseen and having it shipped to you by air. This is not complicated and is done frequently in the reptile world. When the time comes, your breeder can explain to you the mechanics of receiving your pet via air shipment.

ATTEND A HERP SHOW

Herp expositions, where breeders display their wares, are frequently held all over the country. To locate a herp show, where you're bound to find lots of geckos for sale, check the listings in reptile-related magazines (see chapter 10).

There are several ways to find a breeder. Start by trying to get a personal referral from a friend, relative or acquaintance who has done business with the breeder. You can also contact a reptile association (see chapter 10) and ask for a referral. Check advertisements in reptile magazines or newsletters, call a local reptile veterinarian or do a search on the Internet.

Eventually, you will have the name and phone numbers of several breeders. Unless you have a personal reference from someone who has purchased a gecko from the breeders you are considering, ask the breeders for some references. Call these people and ask them about how they were treated before and after they purchased their gecko and how their pets are faring. If you get positive information from these references, chances are you have chosen a responsible, quality breeder.

A responsible gecko breeder can help you decide which species is best suited for your lifestyle and the climate you live in. (Giant Day Gecko)

Choosing the Right Gecko for You

Now that you know where to go to get your gecko, what exactly should you look for when you are picking out your pet (or asking your breeder to select one for you)?

SPECIES

Your first and most important consideration is the species of geckos. There are over 700 species of geckos in the world. Not all of them are available in the pet trade, but a good many are. There are 20 species profiled in this book (see chapter 7, "Types of Geckos"), and there are also rarer kinds available. You will need to research these different species to figure out which ones are most appealing to you and easiest to care for. Do your homework and get to know the needs of the species you like.

If you are new to gecko keeping, your wisest move would be to choose one of the more common, easily kept geckos. While some of the more brightly colored or uniquely shaped species might appeal to you, these are often difficult to care for, and even more difficult to find. Once you gain experience in gecko ownership, you can always add another more exotic species to your collection later on. If you select an "easy keeper" now, you are more likely to have a happy and successful experience with gecko ownership.

CAPTIVE-BRED OR WILD-CAUGHT?

Another point to consider when thinking about species is whether you prefer a captive-bred or wild-caught animal. Captive-bred geckos are generally healthier, live longer and are usually free from parasites. Unlike wild-caught specimens, they don't require an acclimation period and are usually easier to care for. Captive-bred geckos also come guilt-free to those who don't like the idea of taking a wild animal from its home.

On the other hand, only a few gecko species are bred in captivity, and you will be limiting yourself significantly if you choose to only purchase a captive-bred lizard.

WHAT ABOUT CLIMATE?

When determining which species to select, you should also take your geographic location into consideration. If you live in a warm, arid climate, you will find care of a desert or semi-arid species the easiest. Species that hale from desert climates need very little humidity, and your local air temperature won't be much different from the gecko's natural environment. On the other hand, if you live in a hot, humid area, a desert-dwelling species will be harder to maintain. You'll need to watch the humidity and temperature in your pet's terrarium to make sure it is right for your pet.

Time is another factor to consider when choosing a species. If you don't anticipate being home a lot, one of the more demanding tropical species that needs regular misting with water may not be a good choice. On the other hand, if you plan to spend a lot of time at home caring for your new lizard (and don't anticipate the situation changing in the future), you may be in the position to acquire a more care-intensive species.

HEALTH

It's important to start out on the right foot by selecting a gecko that is in good health. A gecko's general health can be determined in a number of ways. First, take a look at its eyes. They should be bright, and in the case of lidded geckos, they should be wide open. The eyes should be clear, with no discharge in the corners. If the gecko is awake, its eyes should not be sunken in.

Look at the gecko's nostrils, too. Check to see if they are clean and free of discharge. The mouth should also look neat, without sores or loose tissue. It should be closed if the animal is relaxed. Geckos with mouths constantly held slightly open often have a respiratory ailment.

The gecko's body should not be too thin for its species. You should not see any ribs or other bones under the skin. All the toes and claws (depending on the species) should be intact and look healthy. Geckos sometimes get infected feet when they don't adequately shed all their skin, with old skin bunched around the toes.

> ### SIGNS OF GOOD HEALTH
>
> The gecko you choose should be in the best of health. Here's what to look for:
>
> - Clear eyes (free of discharge)
> - Clean nostrils (free of discharge)
> - Closed, clean mouth
> - Well-developed body (not bony)
> - Intact toes and claws (free of infection)
> - Alert and active

Attitude is also important when determining a gecko's health. Look for an animal that is alert and active. While nocturnal species will seem a bit listless during the day, if they are stimulated, they should perk up and look wide awake. Learn about the behavioral habits of the species in which you are interested, and observe the individual geckos you are considering to see if they are behaving normally.

Be sure to take notice of the gecko's enclosure. Is it clean and relatively odor-free? Are all the other animals kept in spacious, adequately set-up enclosures? Do the other geckos in the facility appear healthy? (This is important because certain gecko ailments are contagious.) Are there just the right amount of geckos in the enclosure? A gecko that has been subjected to overcrowding is more susceptible to illness.

If you plan on keeping more than one gecko, keep in mind that males are territorial and should be housed separately from other males. (White-Lined Geckos)

Examine the gecko for external parasites such as ticks and mites. These pests lodge themselves under a gecko's scales, and can be seen most clearly on the underside of the animal, often near the base of the tail. Mites will look like small brown or red spots, while ticks will appear as lumps under the skin. Notice if the other geckos in the enclosure are plagued by these pests. Even if the individual you are considering does not appear to have mites or ticks, if the other geckos in the tank do, yours probably has them as well.

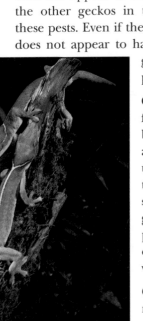

Check the gecko's enclosure for fecal matter. The stool should be firm, and will sometimes be accompanied by a white strip of urea. A small damp area around the stool is normal, but if the stool is watery, watch out: The gecko probably has digestive problems. Another sign of this is crusty stool around the gecko's vent, just under the tail.

Consider taking an experienced reptile keeper along with you on your quest to select a gecko. A trained eye can be very valuable as you are trying to determine the health and general status of an individual animal.

GENDER

The sex of the gecko you buy is only important if you plan to breed the animal, or if you plan to house it with other geckos. Male geckos are territorial and should be kept alone or with one or two females. Sexual characteristics differ among species, and the breeder or a reptile store employee can help you determine the gender of the individual you are considering.

A healthy gecko will have bright eyes that are clear and wide open. (Geckonia chazalie)

AGE

Age is not a very important factor when buying a gecko, although you don't want an animal that is too old because you want to have it around for awhile! On the other hand, while baby geckos are cute, they are also more fragile and prone to ailments.

chapter 4

Housing Your Gecko

How you house your gecko is probably the single most important factor in determining whether you succeed in gecko ownership. The right enclosure with the correct substrate, temperature and humidity levels can make the difference between a happy, healthy gecko and one that is short lived.

Housing Considerations

In order to set up the proper housing and environment for your pet, you first need to understand the needs of the particular species you have chosen to keep. Study the natural range and environment of the animal you plan to purchase, and then do your best to provide a similar habitat. This is easy to do once you know where the species originally came from.

Also be sure you do your homework and your shopping long before you actually bring your gecko home. You should have the enclosure completely set up and ready to be inhabited before your new pet arrives.

A word of advice while you are planning: Don't keep different gecko species together in the same enclosure, even if the species you have chosen have similar habitat requirements. Geckos are notoriously territorial, and you are asking for trouble if you mix more than one species in a small space.

Your gecko's enclosure should be a close recreation of its natural environment. (Leopard Gecko)

SIZE

First, consider the size of the enclosure. The more room you can provide for your gecko, the better. Buy your gecko the largest enclosure that your allotted space and your wallet will accommodate. Giving your gecko plenty of room in which to move around will help it stay happy and healthy. Don't forget: Geckos are basically wild animals that, in nature, have freedom to move around as they please. The closer you can come to recreating a natural environment for your pet, the better off it will be.

When determining suitable living space for a gecko, keep your pet's species in mind. Do your research, and find out what the minimum space requirements are for the type of gecko you have chosen. As a general rule, smaller geckos can be housed comfortably in smaller enclosures. However, you also need to take into consideration the activity level of the species.

Population is another important factor to consider. If you plan to house more than one gecko together, then you may need to provide a bigger enclosure. Overcrowding creates stress for the animals and can make them prone to illness. It can also encourage fighting.

When considering cage size, you'll also want to make sure that your enclosure is big enough to accommodate all the accessories that your pet will need to be comfortable. Hiding places, climbing areas (in the case of arboreal species), a water dish and other natural items are all necessities that must be included in your pet's new home.

ENCLOSURES

Most reptile hobbyists house their geckos in reptile terrariums. These can be made from all glass, or glass with a frame. The great thing about these types of terrariums is that they are designed specifically with reptiles in mind and often have features that make care and maintenance easy. Some of these features include tops that are half glass and half screen (on horizontally designed terrariums), holes for light wiring to run through, and covers that can accommodate different types of lighting.

When selecting your terrarium, make sure to choose a design that will best accommodate your species of choice. Remember that terrestrial species need a horizontally designed terrarium, while arboreal species should thrive in an enclosure that is tall and vertically oriented.

You may have an old aquarium that you would prefer to use. If your gecko is a terrestrial species, all you'll need to do is purchase a screen top as a cover. Make sure the top is secure because some gecko species are notorious escape artists. If you have an arboreal species, you can use the aquarium by turning it on its end. You'll then need to make a door of some kind so you have access to the inside of the tank. Your best bet is to construct a half-door, possibly made of screen. The other half should be made of glass.

You can also build your own terrarium. Use glass and screen as your foundation materials, and remember to design something that will be easy to clean.

Whatever you end up using as an enclosure for your gecko, remember that good ventilation is important to your pet's health. Don't select or build a terrarium that will not allow adequate air flow, or your pet will undoubtedly suffer.

A suitable living space for your gecko includes adequate ventilation, leg room and space for all necessary accessories. (Leopard Gecko)

LIGHTING

The type of lighting you choose for your gecko depends solely on the species you are housing. Most geckos are nocturnal and therefore do not require significant lighting. If your terrarium is in a room where it receives a lot of natural light, your gecko will sense when it is nighttime and when it is daytime. If your pet's enclosure is in a part of the house where there is little natural light, you will have to provide artificial light to mimic night and day. Be careful not to place your terrarium in an area where it will receive direct sunlight. Heat from the sun filtered through glass can warm the interior of the terrarium to deadly temperatures.

The best means of providing light for nocturnal species is with standard incandescent lighting. During daylight hours, use a white or clear 60-watt bulb, and leave it on for as long as the sun is up, as long as it doesn't raise the cage temperature beyond recommended levels. (There are exceptions to this; certain species require more light because of the part of the world where they originated.)

If you are also using this light as your pet's only source of heat, then during the colder months you will need to turn on a red or blue incandescent light during the night. The colored light will not register with your gecko, and so it will behave as if in darkness. Meanwhile, the bulb will still provide heat to the enclosure. An added bonus is that you will be able to watch your pet's nocturnal activities.

Terrariums should have a heat source as well as a much cooler spot—your gecko will regulate its temperature by alternating between the two. (New Caledonia Crested Gecko)

If you choose to go this route, you can purchase a terrarium cover with two separate light sockets and individual switches, which will allow you to alternate between white light and colored light.

Be sure that your incandescent light is focused only on one area of the terrarium and that the enclosure is big enough to provide a temperature gradient. This means that while it may be very warm just under the light, the area opposite from the heat source should be significantly cooler. If you do not provide a substantial temperature gradient, the excessive heat could kill your gecko.

Geckos that are diurnal (active during the day) need very different lighting from their nocturnal cousins. For these pets, you must supply full-spectrum lighting designed specifically for reptiles. This type of lighting mimics the sun and allows the gecko's body to manufacture the nutrients it needs to stay healthy. It will also be necessary if the plants in your terrarium are to survive.

Do not place a full-spectrum bulb over a glass top be-cause the glass will filter out some of the bulb's beneficial properties. Remember, be sure to provide a temperature gradient within the diurnal gecko's terrarium. Allow your pet to be able to escape the heat source and cool its body when needed.

Heat

All geckos need to have heat provided to them during colder periods because they are unable to manufacture body heat internally as mammals and birds do. There are several methods for adding heat to your terrarium.

The type of heat source you choose should depend on the species of gecko you are housing. Most nocturnal geckos prefer to heat themselves by lying on a warm area of substrate (this is called thigmothermic). A spot light can work for these lizards, as can under-tank heating pads. Heating elements called hot rocks are also available, but many experts advise against using them because they can become too hot and subsequently burn the lizard. Many enthusiasts use them regardless, so if you do, exercise extreme caution.

If you use an under-tank heating pad or a spot light, be sure to leave a large area of the terrarium cool so the gecko can get out of the heat if it needs to.

> ### BEWARE OF HOT ROCKS
>
> "Hot rocks" are found in pet supply stores and are designed to provide reptiles with a simple way to thermoregulate. Lizards and snakes, unfortunately, don't always know when they should move away from a hot rock and have been known to burn themselves badly. Other heat sources are safer for your pet, so if you choose to include a hot rock in your gecko's enclosure, monitor the heat emitted—and your pet's behavior—very carefully.

For diurnal geckos, spot lighting is best because these lizards prefer to bask in order to obtain their necessary light and warmth (they are what's known as helio-thermic). Use full-spectrum lighting (perhaps in tandem with an incandescent bulb) to warm a basking spot to around 88 to 92°F. Make sure the rest of the terrarium is significantly cooler so the gecko can regulate its body temperature.

To keep diurnal geckos warm at night when the light is off, you may want to consider heat tapes or under-tank heating pads. Again, make sure your pet can escape the heat if it needs to.

In the summertime or during warm periods, you may want to cut back on the amount of heat you provide for your gecko, depending on its species. However, with diurnal geckos, don't cut back on the amount of light you provide them because they need it for their health. Simply use a bulb with a lower wattage, or keep your air conditioner running in your home and continue to use your regular heat source.

No matter what type of heat source you provide, you should furnish your gecko's terrarium with a thermometer so you can monitor the heat levels within. Different species require different temperatures, and this is the only effective way to monitor the enclosure. You can use a household thermometer, or purchase one made especially for terrarium use at a pet supply store. Place the thermometer at the end of the terrarium that contains the heat source. If you'd like to be sure that you have supplied your pet with a sufficient temperature gradient, place a second thermometer at the other end of the tank.

HUMIDITY

The humidity, or moisture content of the air, inside your terrarium will affect your gecko's health. Humidity requirements are different for different species, and so you'll need to find out exactly what your chosen gecko needs.

There are several methods to provide humidity to a gecko's terrarium. For species that come from arid environments, an occasional misting with water is all that is needed. For tropical species, however, you will need to provide a lot more moisture.

One way to create a humid environment in your tropical gecko's enclosure is to use an aquarium heater and submerge it in a glass container filled with water. As the water heats and evaporates, it will add moisture to the air.

Regular misting with water is another way to keep the air humid in your terrarium, although you shouldn't spray it directly on the lizard. Constantly wet scales can cause skin problems, and even geckos from tropical climates prefer to keep their skin dry even though the air is moist.

The inclusion of tropical plants will also boost the humidity inside your gecko's enclosure, as will a dish of water placed at the bottom of the tank. (Make sure the dish is shallow so your gecko can't fall in and drown.) Some good, leafy plants for tropical lizard terrariums include philodendron, bromeliad, spiderwort and peperomia. Keep in mind that it is hard to maintain a high humidity level in enclosures with screen tops. You'll need to find a balance between good ventilation and too much fresh air.

Plants such as philodendron, bromeliad, spiderwort and peperomia will help bolster the humidity level in your Gecko's enclosure. (Trinidad Day Gecko)

Keep track of the level of relative humidity in your gecko's terrarium. Humidity level indicators, similar to thermometers, a usually available at reptile supply stores.

SUBSTRATE

The type of ground matter you provide to your gecko
will depend heavily on the species you have acquired.
Different types of geckos need different types of substrates, depending on the natural habitat in which they
evolved.

For geckos that normally inhabit desert climates, sand
is a good option. However, if you choose this substrate,
be certain that you equip your terrarium only with
fine grain sand. Geckos have been known to ingest
large quantities of sand, and if the grains are too big,
they can cause a fatal blockage in the gecko's digestive
tract.

The safest sand to use is "reptile sand," which is sand
made specifically for use in reptile terrariums. Although this material can be a bit expensive, it is available in different colors and is safe to use with geckos.
If you'd prefer something less expensive, you can purchase ordinary play sand, usually available at lumber
yards or "do-it-yourself" stores.

One of the greatest advantages to sand is that it is easy
to clean. Waste and dead insects can be easily scooped
out with a spoon or small strainer. A disadvantage to
sand is that it can stick to a gecko's feet. If your gecko
has sticky pads on its feet, sand is not a good choice for
a substrate. Sand can also cause skin problems if it gets
under the scales, although this is uncommon.

Bark is another option for many arid-climate geckos,
and it can also be used for many tropical species as
well. Orchid bark is safe for reptiles, as is the kind commercially sold in pet stores specifically for use in reptile
terrariums. Not all bark is safe for use with reptiles, so
make sure the bark you purchase is meant for reptile
enclosures. If you choose to use bark as your substrate,
change soiled areas frequently.

There are several other substrates you can use, depending on the species you have chosen. Some of these
require mixing different materials such as pea gravel,
peat moss, mulch, humus, sand and other materials.

You can even use unprinted newsprint paper with some species, since it is very absorbent. Potting soil that does not contain fertilizers, pesticides, vermiculite, perlite or herbicides can be suitable for tropical, arboreal species. Study the substrate requirements for the species you have chosen, and then create the most natural environment for your pet.

Keep in mind that material for substrates should not be obtained from the great outdoors. The reason for this is that the material, whatever it is, might be harboring dangerous organisms or chemicals.

ACCESSORIES

In addition to the basic components of a good terrarium, you will need to provide your gecko with a number of accessories that will help it stay healthy and comfortable in its new home.

One of your gecko's strongest instincts is to hide, so provide some driftwood, cork wood or polished stone for this purpose. (Leopard Gecko)

Hiding Places

Geckos are predators, but they are also prey. In the wild, geckos have plenty to worry about from other animals. Birds, mammals and even other lizards commonly make meals out of them. This is why geckos—even those in captivity—do so much hiding.

It is very important that you provide your gecko with a secure hiding place. Although you won't be able to see your pet while it is hiding, depriving it of a hiding place will cause it great stress. The need to hide is one of the gecko's strongest instincts.

There are different ways to provide a hiding place for your gecko, depending on the species you have chosen. Most geckos will be happy with a hollowed out piece of cork wood or driftwood that they can tuck themselves under in a self-made cave. There are also commercially made reptile hide boxes, many made from plastic, available in pet stores. These are suitable for ground-dwelling species.

Some gecko species prefer hiding places between rocks. For these geckos, don't just pile a bunch of rocks together. The movement of the gecko can knock the rocks down, and the animal could be crushed. Instead, glue the rocks together and to the foundation of your terrarium, using a non-toxic but strong glue. The safest type of rock to use is polished stone.

Arboreal geckos also need a place to hide. Many species will hide under leaves or between peeling bark and the wood beneath it. Find out what type of shelter your arboreal gecko species prefers, and be sure to provide it.

Plants

In the wild, geckos share their existence with plants, so its only natural that you should provide these in their captive environment. You can plant plants directly in the substrate of your terrarium, or simply place potted plants on top of the substrate. Some species prefer plants that are growing right from the substrate so they can dig burrows around the base of the plant. Study your species of choice and determine which method is best.

If your gecko is a desert species, succulents make good terrarium plants. However, because nocturnal geckos do not need full-spectrum lighting and plants do, you may have trouble growing live plants in a desert terrarium unless you use several fluorescent tubes overhead. There are some very nice artificial cactus and succulents for sale in pet supply stores that have been made specifically for use in reptile terrariums, and you can always opt for one of these. Do not use any artificial or real spiny cactus in your terrarium because your gecko could injure itself. Safe desert plants for lizard terrariums are agave, sedum and aloe.

Tropical arboreal gecko species need plants that they can climb on and hide in. Plants with large, firm leaves that will support the gecko's weight are good choices. Because you'll need to keep the humidity in your tropical gecko's tank rather high, you are best off getting plants that are tropical themselves. They will appreciate the humidity, and with the right full-spectrum lighting, will thrive.

In addition to increasing the humidity level and providing shelter, plants help simulate a natural environment in your gecko's enclosure. (Madagascar Banded Day Gecko)

When choosing plants for your gecko's terrarium, do not buy species that are toxic because this will cause health problems for your lizard. Even though geckos do not consume plant material, their skin comes into contact with the plant, and the toxins can make the gecko ill. Talk to a horticulturist in your area to determine the safest plants for your gecko.

Bowls

Although many gecko species won't drink from a water bowl, you should be cautious and provide one nonetheless. (For those species that won't use a water bowl, the plants in their terrarium must be sprayed daily so they can drink the droplets.) A water bowl will

45

also help increase the humidity in a lizard's terrarium.

You can also place a small aquarium airstone in a shallow bowl of water. It will roil the water, throwing droplets onto nearby plants, encouraging the gecko to drink.

Water bowls for geckos should always be shallow so the lizard can't drown in them. The lid of a food jar will suffice, although there are many different and rather attractive natural-looking reptile water bowls available in pet supply stores. Some of these look like rocks and can be sunken into the substrate for a more natural environment.

Change your gecko's water daily, being sure to rinse out the bowl each time. This will prevent potentially harmful bacteria from building up in the water.

If you plan to feed mealworms and other grubs to your gecko, you may want to consider including a shallow food dish. The mealworms can be placed in the dish and will usually stay put until the gecko decides to eat them. This will prevent them from getting lost in the substrate and help reduce the amount of substrate your gecko ingests when he captures them.

Adding rocks and branches to your gecko's enclosure gives it a natural feel and provides a diversion for your pet. (Namibian Web-footed Gecko)

Decorations

There's not much need for decorative items in your gecko's terrarium. If you'd like, you can add a few rocks or branches here and there so your gecko can climb on or over them. These will help add a nice, natural look to your pet's enclosure, and give your gecko something to do. However, be sure to anchor any rocks to the terrarium foundation with a non-toxic glue so they don't accidentally fall on your gecko should it decide to dig underneath.

Some gecko keepers like to add a backdrop to their pet's enclosure. There are commercially made backdrops available at pet supply stores, featuring desert, woodland and tropical scenes. These backdrops can add to the attractiveness of your terrarium, and even insulate it to help keep heat in. Or, you can simply add a sheet of construction paper or colored tin-foil backgrounds (available at tropical fish stores) to the outside back of the terrarium to add some color to the enclosure.

chapter 5

Feeding Your Gecko

The nutritional needs of some gecko species are relatively easy to meet. With other species, providing a nutritionally complete diet can be more difficult. The key to success in feeding your gecko is to take the time to learn about its dietary requirements. The way you feed your gecko can mean the difference between a healthy, long-lived pet and a sickly animal.

In nature, geckos are opportunistic insectivores, which means they eat just about any insect small enough to swallow that crosses their path. This method of feeding presents geckos with the greatest chance to obtain a variety of vitamins and minerals from the different insect species that they consume.

It is difficult to provide captive geckos with the kind of variety and nutrition that they would naturally find in the wild. However, fervent gecko keepers often spend considerable time trying to do so. If you want your pet to live a long, happy life, do your best to provide your gecko with the best diet possible.

Frequency of Feeding

There is no hard and fast rule that dictates how often to feed your gecko—trial and error is your best bet for determining appropriate feedings.

Note, however, that animals under 6 months of age are growing rapidly and must be fed (and supplemented) every day.

When you are trying to determine how often to feed your adult gecko, begin by offering your pet a feeding of several insects every other day. If the insects are readily consumed at each feeding, you have found a good schedule. However, if some of the insects are ignored by your gecko, and even start dying in the enclosure because they've been in there so long, you'll need to cut back on the amount you are offering.

Vitamins and Minerals

In the wild, geckos usually get all the vitamins and minerals they need to stay healthy. In captivity, however, owners often have to make an extra effort to provide them with these necessities. If they don't, geckos will develop a variety of health problems. In fact, calcium deficiency is a big problem in captive lizards when their diets are not adequately supplemented.

Fortunately for gecko owners, there are a number of vitamin and mineral supplements made especially for reptiles that are readily available in pet stores. These products are usually available in the form of drops or powders and can be added to a gecko's water or meal.

When choosing a supplement for your gecko, make sure the product is specifically made for use in reptiles. It's important to choose a product that indicates there is a balance of calcium, phosphorus and Vitamin D$_3$ contained within.

Because many gecko species won't drink from a water dish and even those that do won't do it with great regularity, your best bet is to "dust" your gecko's meal with the supplement before feeding. You can do this by taking the insects and placing them in a plastic bag or container, along with some of the supplement. Shake gently until the insects are covered with the powder, and feed immediately.

The bad news is that no two experts agree on how often this supplementation should be carried out. Some recommend every feeding, others every other feeding. Most will agree that at least one feeding a week should be supplemented for most gecko species.

What to Feed Your Gecko

CRICKETS

Most gecko species can live on a diet of crickets—dusted with a vitamin and mineral supplement—alone. (Tokay Gecko)

Most captive geckos subsist on a diet of commercially bred insects, primarily crickets. Crickets make a good staple diet, and many gecko species can live on this insect alone, provided the crickets are dusted regularly with a vitamin and mineral supplement. (Make

sure there is always water present in your gecko's enclosure when crickets are placed there for your pet to consume. Crickets that are denied sufficient moisture may try to retrieve it from your gecko's eyes!)

Crickets are readily available at most pet stores and reptile specialty stores. While you can simply buy a dozen crickets or so every week, dust them with a supplement and place them in your gecko's enclosure, it's much better to boost the crickets' nutritional value before feeding them to your pet. This practice is known as "gut loading." Crickets purchased directly from a commercial outlet usually have not eaten in quite some time, and by gut loading you help to ensure that they are nutritious food for your gecko.

It's also a good idea to alternate the food items you feed your crickets to ensure that your gecko is getting a varied diet. For example, provide fish-food flakes at one feeding and commercial cricket food the next.

MEALWORMS

Mealworms, the larval stage of the *Tenebrio molitor* beetle, are another suitable and readily available food item for captive geckos, but in the case of mealworms, too much of a good thing can be harmful.

Your Gecko will enjoy a variety of worms in moderation, easily available from pet shops and through the mail. (Leopard Gecko)

The outer skin of the mealworm contains chitin (a tough substance that is difficult to digest) which, in large doses, is not healthy for your gecko. Therefore, a feeding of several mealworms once a week is enough for your gecko to consume.

Mealworms can usually be purchased in quantities of 50, 100 or more and kept refrigerated until they are served to your lizard. The cold temperature in the refrigerator keeps them in a torpid state and prevents them from developing into beetles.

WAXWORMS

Another feeder insect available at many pet stores is the waxworm, which is actually a caterpillar and the larvae of the wax moth. Because waxworms are high in fat, they should only be fed to your gecko sparingly. Another bit of advice: Don't buy too many of these at once because they lose their nutritional value quickly when not consumed for a few days.

KINGWORMS

Kingworms, or king mealworms as they are sometimes called, can also be fed to some of the larger gecko species since they are rather big: 2½ inches in length. Larvae of the *Zoophobas* beetle, kingworms are usually available at reptile specialty stores. Feed these in moderation because, like mealworms, their outer skin contains chitin.

WILD-CAUGHT INSECTS

The best thing to do is to provide your gecko with as much insect variety as you possibly can. This means, in addition to providing crickets and occasional mealworms, waxworms or kingworms, you should also supply your pet with wild-caught insects such as sow bugs, cockroaches, termites, moths, caterpillars, spiders (non-poisonous varieties), grasshoppers, locusts, houseflies and other small creatures. The rule of thumb is this: If the insect is even a tiny bit smaller than the gecko's head, the lizard will be able to swallow it.

HOW TO GUT LOAD CRICKETS

In order to gut load crickets, you'll need to keep them for at least twenty-four hours before you feed them to your lizard. Place the crickets in a plastic container with holes punched in the lid for air. An old margarine tub will do, or you can purchase one of the commercial cricket containers available at pet stores. Give the crickets food and a crumpled up paper towel or section of egg carton to hide in. Let them feast for at least an entire day before feeding them to your gecko.

Feeding crickets is not as hard as it sounds. Simply provide them with tropical fish food flakes and a slice of orange, a piece of potato or some grated carrots. Or, you can buy commercially made cricket food at your pet store, which is high in vitamins and minerals. It's important to also provide some fresh, moist fruit or vegetables for the crickets at the same time. By healthfully feeding your crickets, they will pass on these nutrients to your gecko when it consumes them.

When you collect insects from outdoors, you must be absolutely certain that you are obtaining them from an area that has not been sprayed with any pesticides or herbicides. Your own property is really the only place you can be completely certain is safe, providing you have not used any chemical products to control insects or weeds.

Keep in mind that if your adult gecko was raised in captivity and only fed crickets, mealworms and other commercially raised insects, it may not eat any of the wild-caught insects that you offer. The reason for this might be that young geckos learn to identify the insects they are regularly fed as prey, and as adults they don't recognize unfamiliar insects as food. You can continue to try offering wild-caught insects in the hopes that your gecko will eventually be willing to sample something new. Or, you can stick to your pet's old favorites, being sure to use a vitamin and mineral supplement once a week.

> **THEY MAY EAT INSECTS—BUT THEY WON'T CHEW 'EM**
>
> Geckos lose their teeth throughout their lifetime, but new teeth simply grow in to replace the old ones. Most lizards, including geckos, have teeth that are cone-shaped. Unlike our teeth, lizard teeth are all the same size and shape. They will use their teeth to hold on to an insect which they then swallow whole.

BABY MICE

Some of the larger gecko species can be fed an occasional newborn baby mouse, called a "pinky," which can be purchased from reptile specialty shops and some pet stores. If you are squeamish about doing this, however, don't worry about it. Your gecko will be just fine subsisting on an insect-protein diet, provided you don't plan to breed it.

Water

Geckos are no different than other living things when it comes to the importance of water. Your gecko, whether it be a desert-dwelling species or a tropical one, needs to have daily access to water.

How you should provide water depends on the species of gecko you are caring for. Some gecko species are happy to lap water from a shallow dish, which can be placed somewhere at the bottom of the terrarium. You can also offer water on a damp sponge if you prefer, since several dry-climate species actually would rather take water in this form. However, you'll need to be vigilant about making sure the sponge is always damp and free of mildew. And never use soap or detergent to clean it.

Some geckos will not drink water out of a bowl, but instead lick condensation from their faces and nearby leaves. For these geckos, regular misting is necessary. (Madagascar Yellow-throated Day Gecko)

Some of the more tropical arboreal gecko species will only drink water from droplets that have formed on leaves. For these geckos, you will have to provide a daily misting of water that allows these droplets to form. (As a safety measure, keep a dish of water in these geckos' terrariums.) Some experts suggest that you place the dish in an elevated spot, possibly in the fork of a branch. Try adding an aquarium airstone to the water as well to make it roil. This will motivate the gecko to drink and will also scatter droplets on surrounding leaves.

chapter 6

Your Gecko's
Health

Having a healthy gecko begins when you select it at the pet store, reptile swap meet or breeder's facility. Examine your prospective pet carefully. Check to see that it's active, eats readily (request to see it being fed) and is otherwise behaving normally. Examine the eyes and nasal region for signs of mucus or discharge. Ask to hold the gecko that you've selected. Turn it over and observe the anal vent. It should be free of any fecal matter or adherences. Examine the skin for the presence of ticks, or mites, any areas of dry or flaky, unshed skin and sores

or ulcerations. If any of the above conditions are present, it's recommended that you stay away from the animal regardless of how much you may be attracted to it.

Geckos that are kept in optimal conditions rarely get sick. However, your gecko may become susceptible to a variety of illnesses and conditions. If you can recognize the problem early on, you may be able to prevent the condition from becoming worse, and you may even save your gecko's life. If your gecko does get sick, it is your responsibility to take it to a veterinarian as soon as possible.

Selecting a Veterinarian

Before you bring your gecko home, get the name and phone number of a nearby reptile veterinarian and keep it handy in case of an emergency with your lizard. Make sure the veterinarian you select is one who has considerable experience caring for reptiles because this type of animal has significantly different medical needs from those of mammals. Veterinarians who advertise as treating "exotics" are usually experienced with reptiles.

If you are having trouble locating a reptile veterinarian in your area, call your closest reptile specialty shop and ask for a referral. Or, you can contact a national or regional herpetological society (see chapter 10) and ask if they can recommend a reptile veterinarian in your area.

Prevention

The single most important factor in providing for your gecko's health is prevention. Taking action to keep your gecko healthy will reduce the chances of illness and visits to the veterinarian. To help ensure your gecko's good health, there are certain steps you need to take:

- Keep your gecko's enclosure sanitary. Promptly remove waste, dead insects and soiled substrate. Rinse out your pet's water bowl every day. Clean rocks, wood and other items once a month by washing them with a solution of one part bleach to four parts water, and dry them thoroughly in the sun before returning them to the terrarium.

- Provide the appropriate amount of heat, light and humidity for the species you are caring for. Use a thermometer and hygrometer to determine whether you are providing the correct amounts of heat and humidity.

- Feed your pet a variety of nutritious insects at least once a week. The insects should be dusted with a vitamin and mineral supplement that is made especially for reptiles.

- Handle your gecko only as much as absolutely necessary. Too much handling can damage the skin and make your lizard prone to infection. Over-handling also can cause stress in your gecko, which can lower your pet's resistance to disease.

> ## BE AWARE OF SALMONELLA
>
> All victims of a salmonella outbreak in Denver, Colorado, had a few things in common which pointed to reptiles as the source of the infection. They all visited the Denver Zoo, all had eaten finger food there (hot dogs, hamburgers or sandwiches) and all had touched or pressed up against the railing of the Komodo Dragon Lizard *(Varanus komodiensis)* exhibit. The same serotype of salmonella that these victims had was cultured off the railing. This proved that even surfaces touched by the reptile could be responsible for salmonella infection.

- Provide your gecko with a natural environment. Give it a place to hide and allow it to perform normal behaviors. Keep hiding places and furnishings in the same positions within the terrarium to avoiding upsetting your pet.

A Word About Handling

Geckos should not be handled frequently. Excessive handling results in stress, which breaks down the body's defenses. However, sometimes you will need to handle your gecko, most likely when you need to move it to a temporary holding tank when cleaning its enclosure.

When handling your gecko, avoid touching it directly. The gecko's delicate skin could tear, and in the case of aggressive species like the Tokay Gecko, you could also be injured. Instead, try to usher the gecko into a lidded container that you can use to transport it to its temporary enclosure.

If you must hold the gecko in your hand, gently grasp the base of its head between your thumb and forefinger while you support the weight of its body with your palm.

Some of the more docile species, such as the Leopard Gecko, may simply crawl onto your hand if you hold it flat. Avoid grasping the gecko because this may encourage struggling. Instead, place your other hand over your flat hand, and gently put the gecko in the temporary enclosure.

Help keep your gecko healthy by handling it only when absolutely necessary. (Dwarf Frog-Eyed Gecko)

Because human contamination with *Salmonella* bacteria has been occasionally linked to the handling of reptiles, wash your hands thoroughly with an antibacterial soap and warm water immediately after handling your gecko.

Health Problems

If you follow the advice above, chances are you won't have any problems with your gecko. However, should you run across one of the following conditions, treat it yourself as indicated, or contact your veterinarian.

EXTERNAL PARASITES

There are two ectoparasites that can plague geckos: ticks and mites. These pests are usually a problem only in wild-caught geckos, although some lizards can become infested when kept in a pet store or a wholesaler's facility.

Ticks are problematic to geckos because they can cause anemia, spread disease or cause a bacterial infection. Ticks usually lodge in the softest skin of the gecko and so can usually be found where the limbs join the body, in addition to underneath the base of the tail. You can remove ticks by dabbing them with alcohol using a cotton swab and then pulling them out with tweezers. You must be absolutely sure to remove the tick's mouthparts; leaving them behind will usually result in infection. Once the tick is removed, flush it down the toilet.

Mites, on the other hand, are much smaller (tinier than the head of a pin) and jump on and off of the gecko. They live in the lizard's enclosure and feed off the animal at will. Mites are harmful to geckos because they can cause anemia and bacterial infections.

You can remove mites using the alcohol and tweezers described for the removal of ticks, or you can buy commercial reptile mite treatment at your local reptile specialty store. To treat mites in the environment, place a small piece of fly strip on top of the screen of your terrarium for several days. The mites will be drawn to it and will become trapped. Be sure to change your gecko's water several times a day while you are using the fly strip because the chemicals from the strip will contaminate the water.

Wild-caught geckos should be examined by a veterinarian for internal parasites as well as for ticks and mites. (Namib Geckos)

Use only a small amount of fly strip, preferably a piece that is about two inches long. Use caution when handling the strip as it contains insecticides. Wear gloves and wash your hands immediately after handling a fly strip.

INTERNAL PARASITES

Geckos born in captivity typically have few problems with internal parasites, such as amoebas, tapeworms, threadworms, coccidia, flukes and roundworms. However, wild-caught geckos frequently harbor these organisms, and occasionally a captive-bred lizard can be afflicted with them. Signs of internal parasites include diarrhea, poor appetite and a lethargic appearance.

An infestation of internal parasites must be treated by your veterinarian. Bring a sample of your gecko's stool to your veterinarian's office to be analyzed. The exact parasite will be determined, and the veterinarian will prescribe medication you can give your pet at home.

WOUNDS AND ABSCESSES

Keep your gecko free of wounds and abscesses by housing it in a safe enclosure that is not overcrowded. Check objects kept in the enclosure for sharp edges. Separate aggressive geckos from the rest of the terrarium inhabitants. If geckos fight (especially the more aggressive species), wounds and abscesses may result.

Ample humidity in your gecko's enclosure will help your pet shed a top layer of skin every few weeks. (Madagascar Spotted Day Gecko)

If an injury occurs, swab Betadine™ solution or an antibiotic ointment on the affected area. Call your veterinarian and ask for an appointment to have your gecko examined and treated.

Geckos sometimes lose their tails during fights and if frightened or accidentally dropped. If this happens, swab the area with Betadine™ solution or an antibiotic ointment and isolate the gecko. Provide an ample amount of food, and keep the gecko separated until the wound heals. (Be aware that the tail will never grow back completely.)

Keeping the substrate in your gecko's enclosure clean will help reduce the occurrence of skin infections. (White-Eyed Gecko)

SHEDDING DIFFICULTIES

It is normal for geckos to shed a top layer of skin every few weeks or so. However, a gecko can have trouble losing its skin if the amount of humidity in its enclosure isn't just right. This stubborn skin has a tendency to linger most often on the gecko's toes.

Allow your gecko several hours to shed the skin completely. If patches of skin still linger after several days, place the gecko in a plastic container with some damp paper towels at the bottom. Punch holes in the lid, and keep the gecko warm and confined in the container for at least an hour.

It is normal for your gecko to ingest its shedding skin. This provides the lizard with valuable nutrients. Allow the gecko to do this without being disturbed. Leave the excess pieces of skin that end up in the substrate because many geckos will consume them within a day or so. If the skin is left for longer than three days, feel free to remove the skin from the enclosure.

MOUTH ROT

Some geckos, like other reptiles, are prone to a bacterial ailment called "mouth rot," or infectious stomatitis. It is usually the result of an injury to the mouth area or poor nutrition, and it often takes the form of a pus-like discharge around the outside of the mouth. The gecko may refuse to eat. If not treated early, the bacteria can spread to the inside of the mouth and cause serious problems. If you suspect your gecko has mouth rot, take it to a veterinarian immediately.

A balanced diet, including sufficient calcium, helps prevent bone disease in young geckos. (Adult captive Leopard Gecko and hatchling)

SKIN INFECTIONS

Geckos that are kept on dirty substrate can develop skin infections on the underside of their bodies. The infected tissue looks like a brown or black blemish.

If your gecko has a skin infection, provide it with clean substrate immediately. Put Betadine™ solution or antibiotic cream on the affected areas, and contact your veterinarian right away.

DIARRHEA

Problems with your gecko's digestive system will most likely result in diarrhea, bloody stool or green stool. Contact your veterinarian immediately. If diarrhea is left untreated, the lizard can quickly become dehydrated and die. A number of different or-ganisms and problems can cause digestive ailments. Bring a stool sample to your veterinarian so he or she can determine if a parasite is responsible for the situation.

METABOLIC BONE DISEASE

Geckos that are deprived of sufficient calcium can develop metabolic bone disease. This condition is most common in young geckos that are still growing. Signs of metabolic bone disease include deformed limbs and general weakness.

If the disease has not progressed severely, the reptile's life can be saved by changing its diet to include sufficient calcium (although deformities developed during growth cannot be changed). Contact your veterinarian for advice if you suspect that your gecko has metabolic bone disease.

Geckos

Close-Up

Types of Geckos

Geckos are a family within the reptile class, therefore all gecko species have a number of traits in common. However, if you take a close look at the different species within the gecko family, you'll see that geckos can differ significantly from one to another.

There are approximately 700 different gecko species in the world, but most species are not regularly kept in captivity. The following discussion will examine the gecko species you are most likely to find available.

Leopard Gecko

EUBLEPHARIS MACULARIUS

The most popular gecko in North America is the Leopard Gecko. This handsome lizard with an easy-going temperament is by far the easiest gecko to keep and breed in captivity. With proper care, they can live to be 20 years old.

Leopard Geckos are not wild-caught, they are bred exclusively for the purpose of being kept as pets. For those who prefer not to own an animal that was taken from the wild, a Leopard Gecko is an excellent choice.

Origins

The Leopard Gecko is a member of the *Eublepharinae* subfamily of geckos. It evolved in the arid lands of Southwest Asia and can be found in the wild in Iran, Afghanistan, Pakistan and India. Most of the Leopard Geckos in the United States descended from geckos that were originally imported from Pakistan.

Leopard Gecko

Appearance

Leopard Geckos are about 3½ inches at birth and can grow to a length of approximately 8 to 12 inches within 1½ years, and they are one of the largest of all gecko species. Their bodies are flat and cylindrical shaped, and their heads are large. They typically have sandy white or pale yellow skin with irregular dark purple spots on the upper portion of their heads and backs— hence their name. Their tails are usually lighter in color with pale-purple bands. Juvenile Leopard Geckos have dark bands across their entire bodies. These bands slowly fade as the gecko matures and are replaced by the traditional leopard-like spots. The scales on Leopard Gecko bodies are granular, meaning they are small and flat in appearance.

Because Leopard Geckos are so easy to breed, they have become a favorite subject of breeders who are trying develop new gecko colors. Variant color strains of Leopard Geckos are available from commercial breeders—some are nearly all yellow with no spots, or bright yellow with dark spots and even yellow with stripes instead of spots. These geckos are considerably more expensive and harder to find than conventional Leopard Geckos. They usually have to be purchased directly from a breeder.

As typical members of the *Eublepharinae* subfamily, Leopard Geckos possess movable eyelids. They also lack the adhesive toe pads found on many other gecko species, and so are primarily terrestrial. They do have small claws that give them good traction and enable them to climb on rocks and other objects. Healthy Leopard Geckos have a thick tail and a long, pink tongue with a notch in the center. Their ears are quite prominent—if you hold a Leopard Gecko up to the light, you can see right through its ears.

Behavior

The Leopard Gecko is popular largely due to its gentle nature. Unlike other species, Leopard Geckos rarely bite, and when they do, their bite is painless. For this reason, they are easy to handle.

Leopard Geckos are nocturnal, which means they are most active at night. Although they spend much of the day sleeping in a hiding place, Leopard Geckos will occasionally emerge during the day. However, they are most active in the evening when they come out to hunt and consume crickets and mealworms. If they are exposed to other bugs when youngsters, geckos will also eat other insect prey.

Male Leopard Geckos tend to be territorial and will fight with other males. They will also court females who are kept in the same terrarium. Female Leopard

Geckos can be aggressive toward other species of geckos and may be better off in a separate enclosure.

Care

Leopard Geckos are the easiest geckos to care for. An adult Leopard Gecko can live in a 10-gallon terrarium, although some experts believe a 20-gallon enclosure is a better choice, particularly if you are housing more than one gecko. They will typically use only one corner of their enclosure to defecate and urinate, making them easy to clean up after.

Fine reptile sand, bark, reptile carpet or even newspaper is suitable substrate for Leopard Gecko terrariums. A shallow dish should be provided for water. Because Leopard Geckos will also eat a calcium supplement out of a dish, this can be kept in the terrarium as well.

Because Leopard Geckos evolved in a warm, dry climate, they need a regular heat source when the weather is cool. Heat pads are one way to provide this. Some keepers use heat lamps instead, although Leopard Geckos don't typically bask under these lights because of their nocturnal behavior. However, if your pet's terrarium is in an area where it receives little natural light, you may want to consider providing an incandescent light source during the day and a red bulb at night. It's best to maintain the daytime temperature at around 85°F and the evening temperature at 75°F. Make sure that there are cool areas in the terrarium so your lizard can regulate its body temperature, as well as hiding places where it can sleep.

If you live in a dry climate, spray a light mist of water in an area of the terrarium near the gecko's hide box every few days to help your Leopard Gecko shed its skin. If you live in a climate that tends to be damp, make sure your terrarium has a screen top so moisture won't get trapped inside.

Leopard Geckos can live happily on a diet of crickets and mealworms. If you do not provide a dish of calcium supplement in your Leopard Gecko's enclosure, be sure to dust the crickets with the supplement every third feeding. You can try feeding your gecko an occasional waxworm or kingworm, or even a sow bug or spider from your yard, provided you do not use pesticides. Leopard Geckos that have grown up eating only crickets and mealworms will most likely refuse other types of insects. Feed your Leopard Gecko crickets every other day and mealworms once a week. Other prey can be added to your gecko's diet occasionally.

African Fat-Tailed Gecko

HEMITHECONYX CAUDICINCTUS

African Fat-Tailed Geckos make good pets, much like their cousin the Leopard Gecko. This species is typically captured in Africa and imported here. While environmentally conscious reptile keepers have ethical problems with this issue, this is not the only problem: Captured specimens are often ill and don't survive long in their new home. However, if and when an African Fat-Tailed Gecko survives the transition, it makes a fairly hardy pet.

African Fat-Tailed Gecko

Origins

As their name suggests, the African Fat-Tailed Gecko originated in Africa, in the dry western region of the continent. These geckos are found most commonly in scrub and grassland areas from Nigeria east to Cameroon. They are part of the *Eublepharinae* subfamily of geckos.

Appearance

African Fat-Tailed Geckos are usually pale yellow with dark bands across their bodies and tails. Some variants in the species have a white line that runs along their backbone. Their bodies have a shape similar to the Leopard Gecko's, and yes, they do have fat tails. They also have movable eyelids. African Fat-Tailed Geckos grow to be about 8 inches long.

Behavior

African Fat-Tailed Geckos are easy-going but tend to be shyer than Leopard Geckos. Although they are nocturnal, they will occasionally come out in the daylight. During the day, African Fat-Tailed Geckos prefer to hide under a piece of driftwood or other object. They typically use one area of their terrarium as a bathroom, making it easy to clean. They will hunt and consume crickets, mealworms and other small insects.

Males will fight if placed in close contact with each other, so housing male African Fat-Tailed Geckos together is not recommended.

Care

Wild-caught Fat-Tailed Geckos prefer big terrariums. A 20-gallon enclosure for a single gecko or a pair of geckos is best.

This species will thrive if kept on a bark substrate. They also prefer some humidity, so spraying the terrarium with water a few times a week is recommended. A shallow dish filled with drinking water should also be kept in the gecko's enclosure.

A regular heat source is needed for African Fat-Tailed Geckos, which prefer a temperature of 85°F during the day and 75°F at night. Heating pads are good sources of heat for these reclusive liz-ards. Make sure you provide hiding places in both the warm side of the terrarium and the cooler side so the gecko can regulate its body temperature. If you are keeping this type of gecko in an area of your home where its enclosure receives little light, provide an incandescent light source during the day and a red bulb in the evening. No heating pad will be necessary if you use these bulbs, as they provide a considerable source of heat on their own.

African-Fat Tailed Geckos thrive on a diet consisting primarily of crickets, dusted with a calcium and vitamin supplement every third feeding. An occasional feeding of mealworms should also be given. Wild-caught African Fat-Tailed Geckos are accustomed to eating many different kinds of insects, so you can offer an occasional spider, sow bug or other small insect from your yard, provided you don't use pesticides.

Recently captured African Fat-Tails need time to get accustomed to captivity. Help your gecko acclimate during this transitional period (generally about two months) by keeping it separate from other geckos, providing it with food and water, and keeping it warm at 85°F. If the animal won't eat or seems to be losing weight, take it to your reptile veterinarian.

Banded Gecko
COLEONYX VARIEGATUS

The Banded Gecko is a species native to North America. The Banded Gecko is a symbol of the West and serves as the model for the stylized gecko image seen in Southwestern art.

Origins

A member of the *Eublepharinae* subfamily, the Banded Gecko evolved in the deserts of Southern California, Nevada, Utah, Arizona, New Mexico and Mexico. There are a number of subspecies of this group, each found exclusively in these different areas.

Appearance

Banded Geckos measure in at around 6 inches long. Their bodies are slight, but their tails are somewhat thicker. As its name suggests, this species has bands across its body that start at its head and go all the way to the tip of its tail. These bands start out as distinct markings in juveniles and then become more erratic in design with age. The base color is usually a light tan or yellow, with dark brown bands. The skin of the Banded Gecko contains granular scales and is smooth and fragile.

Banded Gecko

Like their cousins in the *Eublepharinae* subfamily, Banded Geckos have movable eyelids. They also have tiny claws that allow them to climb on rocks, small plants and wood.

Behavior

Like many desert dwellers, the Banded Gecko is nocturnal. This lizard spends much of the hotter daylight hours sleeping under a rock or piece of wood. In captivity, the Banded Gecko follows the same pattern, although sometimes it ventures out during the day.

Male Banded Geckos may fight and so should be kept in separate enclosures. Males and females get along, however, and can be housed together. Be prepared to care for eggs and subsequent young if you keep a male and female in the same terrarium.

In their native environment, Banded Geckos spend time climbing on rocks and the woody remains of dead plants. Be sure to provide objects in the enclosure for your gecko to climb on.

Care

A single adult Banded Gecko can live in a 10-gallon terrarium, although it is best to give your lizard the largest terrarium that you can provide.

Fringe-Toed
Sand Gecko

Banded Geckos are most at home on fine reptile sand, but can also be kept on bark or reptile carpet. They will drink water from a shallow dish, which should also be provided. A hiding place, a rock to crawl over and

some real or artificial desert plants provide a comfortable home for a Banded Gecko.

Because they are desert creatures, these lizards need a warm climate in their terrariums. A heat source in cooler weather will be necessary. If you opt for incandescent light, be sure to use a red bulb in the evening hours so your gecko will not be confused about what time of day it is.

Maintain your Banded Gecko at around 85°F during the day and 75°F at night. Make sure that your gecko can move away from the heat source if it wants to.

Although the desert is typically dry during the day, the evenings can be moist. Therefore, your Banded Gecko will need some humidity to help it shed its skin. If you live in an arid climate, spray the inside of its terrarium with a light mist of water every evening, and keep a cup of moist substrate in the terrarium. However, don't let the terrarium get too damp; make sure you have a screen top that will allow moisture to evaporate.

Banded Geckos can be fed crickets and mealworms, dusted every third feeding with a vitamin and mineral supplement. You can also offer other small insects to your Banded Gecko, provided the bugs come from a yard free of pesticides.

Sand Gecko

CHONDRODACTYLUS ANGULIFER

This gecko species is both hearty and unusual in appearance. The males and females differ from one another in the way they look (dimorphic). Because captive-bred specimens are usually poor breeders, many of the Sand Geckos available are wild-caught. Although European herp keepers often have access to stock, they are difficult to find in the United States.

Origins

Sand Geckos are a member of the *Gekkoninae* subfamily of geckos. They hail from southwestern Africa and are seen from Namibia south to Cape Town, South Africa. Their habitat consists of dry savanna and desert terrain.

Appearance

The adult length of most Sand Geckos is around 7 inches. In nature, their sandy-colored skin helps them blend into the dry terrain in which they live. The base color is a light tan, and wide, v-shaped bands cross their bodies. They have special scales on their feet that enable them to move efficiently over sandy terrain.

Male Sand Geckos are easy to distinguish from females. The males have white spots on their backs and tend to be larger than females. Females will have a greater number of bands on their tails and do not have white spots. Neither sex has movable eyelids, but both have a heavy lid—a sort of built-in sun shade—over each eye.

Behavior

Sand Geckos are most active at night, only venturing forth occasionally during the day. Even when Sand Geckos do come out of their hiding places, they are somewhat sedentary.

The males of this species are territorial and will make clicking noises when scrapping with other males. Rather than risk injury to either party, it's best to keep males of this species in separate enclosures.

Care

Because Sand Geckos are not very active in captivity, a single specimen can exist in a 10-gallon enclosure, although you can provide your pet with more room if you want. If you have more than one of these geckos, supply them with at least a 20-gallon setup.

The best substrate for a Sand Gecko is—you guessed it—sand. You can use reptile sand, or a courser grade if you desire, since this species is adapted to living in this exact type of environment. Sand Geckos need a place to hide during the day, so provide your pet with a burrow of some kind.

Helmeted Geckos

Your desert-dwelling gecko will need a heat source, either a heat pad or incandescent light. Keep the temperature inside the terrarium at 88°F during the day, and drop it down to 78°F at night.

Sand Geckos prefer to drink water that has been sprayed onto surfaces within the terrarium. Do this every other day in addition to providing a shallow dish filled with water.

A diet of crickets with an occasional mealworm makes a good meal for this species. You can also offer your pet other small insects from a pesticide-free garden.

Helmeted Gecko

GECKONIA CHAZALIAE

The Helmeted Gecko somewhat resembles the Horn-ed Lizard (also known commonly as the Horned Toad or Horny Toad) of the American West, but it is much easier to keep. This lizard is somewhat new to the American herp trade but is being bred successfully in captivity and is growing in popularity.

Origins

The Helmeted Gecko was originally found in north-western Africa and is a member of the *Gekkoninae* sub-family. This gecko calls the middle eastern part of the world its home. It is well-suited to the dry desert areas of this part of the African continent.

Appearance

The Helmeted Gecko has a jagged-looking, earth-colored skin tone that helps it blend into the sandy ground of its native land. There are darker, erratic markings scattered around its body.

This lizard's most notable feature is the ridge at the base of its head, which makes it look as if it is wearing a helmet—hence the name. There is also a brow ridge above each lidless eye, which seems to serve as protec-tion from the sun.

One of the smallest gecko species, the Helmeted Gecko only grows to be 4 inches long. Its tail is rather short when compared to that of other gecko species.

Behavior

Originally from a hot environment, the Helmeted Gecko is primarily nocturnal. In some situations, Helmeted Geckos will venture forth from their hiding places dur-ing the day to hunt.

Helmeted Geckos are rather docile and only move quickly when they are feeling threatened. They have been known to make soft clicking noises at times.

As with other species, male Helmeted Geckos are best kept in separate quarters lest they fight over territory.

Care

Because these geckos are so tiny, a 10-gallon terrarium provides sufficient room for one or two individuals.

A combination of heavy sand and light gravel makes a good substrate for these desert dwellers. Reptile sand can also be used. Be sure to provide small hiding places for these lizards, along with a shallow dish for water.

Heat is important to this species, so a heat pad or incandescent light should be provided. The daytime terrarium temperature should range from 85° to 95°F; at night, bring it down to around 75° or 80°F.

Helmeted Geckos will feed on crickets and other small insects. Be sure to dust the insects at every third feeding with a vitamin and mineral supplement.

Tokay Gecko

GEKKO GECKO

The Tokay Gecko, one of the most popular and well-known of all the gecko species, has been a favorite

Tokay Gecko

with reptile keepers for the last few decades. Tokay Geckos have unique characteristics that set them apart from other geckos, one of which is their bold and aggressive temperament. They are readily available in pet shops although most specimens are wild-caught.

Origins

A member of the *Gekkoninae* subfamily, the Tokay Gecko is native to Southeast Asia and traditionally dwells in the rain forests of this region. However, this species can be found wild in the United States, as a result of escaped captives. They have populated a few of the Hawaiian islands and are a common sight in a number of Florida counties.

Appearance

Tokay Geckos are one of the largest members of the gecko family, reaching lengths of up to 14 inches. They are typically pale blue or gray with orange spots covering their bodies. The tail is often banded with the same color pattern.

Tokay Geckos lack movable eyelids and in fact have large protruding eyes that are hard to ignore. Its head is large in proportion to its body, and its feet have adhesive toe pads.

Behavior

Tokay Geckos are well-known for their assertive personality. They are notorious for biting the hand that feeds them and commonly charge at their keepers when they reach into the lizards' enclosures. If they latch onto a finger, they are not inclined to let it go. Their bite is painful and, if administered by a large specimen, can even break the skin. Therefore, it is recommended that Tokay Geckos be approached only with gloved hands.

Another well-known trait of this lizard is its penchant for calling. Both the name "Tokay" and the family name "Gekko" are derived from the sound of this lizard's vocalization.

Tokay Geckos are nocturnal, although they will venture forth from their hiding places during the day. Because they are arboreal (tree-dwelling) lizards, Tokay Geckos will spend most of their time above the ground. In the wild, they are good at seeking out trees with hollow trunks or pieces of loose bark where they can hide.

Male Tokay Geckos are territorial and should not be kept in the same enclosure. Because of this gecko's aggressive nature, fights between males can actually result in death.

Care

Because this species spends little time on the ground, it is best to provide your pet with a terrarium that is vertically designed rather than horizontal. The enclosure should have a screen top for ventilation, with a latch on it so the Tokay cannot escape. A 15-gallon or larger tank will accommodate one Tokay Gecko. Two Tokays should be housed in a 20-gallon or larger tank. It's best to cover one side of the terrarium with some kind of paper because Tokay Geckos feel more secure with only three sides of the terrarium exposed.

Light gravel or wood bark (orchid) makes the best substrate for a Tokay Gecko. Real plants should also be provided in its enclosure because this species lives in heavy foliage in the wild. Provide potted plants with large leaves that the gecko can hide in. If your gecko's terrarium won't be receiving a significant amount of natural light, you'll need to supply artificial light for the plants.

Tokay Geckos need a lot of climbing places in the terrarium to feel secure. Place large pieces of wood in vertical positions in the terrarium for the gecko to climb on.

Humidity is important for this species, so you'll need to provide it with a fairly humid environment. You can do this by keeping the substrate moist by misting it daily. Spray your lizard with the same water, and keep a shallow dish of water in the enclosure. When your Tokay Gecko starts to shed, extra humidity may be necessary.

The temperature in your Tokay Gecko's enclosure should range from approximately 75° to 85°F during the day, and from 65° to 75°F at night. You can use a heat pad or an incandescent light for a heat source. The light will help the plants during the day, but you'll need to switch to a red light in the evenings so your gecko will not be confused into thinking it's daytime around the clock.

Tokay Geckos are voracious eaters, and they can be fed crickets, mealworms, cockroaches, spiders and other insects a few times a week. The insects should be dusted with a vitamin and mineral supplement at least once or twice a week.

House Gecko

HEMIDACTYLUS FRENATUS

If you live in Florida, you've probably seen this little creature hanging around under porches and near street lights, eating insects that come its way. Because of its tendency to live near human dwellings, the House Gecko is one of the better-known gecko species.

Origins

The House Gecko, a member of the *Gekkoninae* subfamily, is originally from Southeast Asia. However, it has been introduced into parts of Africa, Australia and Central America, as well as the southernmost part of the United States. It also sometimes called the Chit-Chat Gecko (because of the noise it makes), the Pacific House Gecko or Asiatic House Gecko.

House Gecko

Appearance

House Geckos grow to be approximately 5 inches long. Their smooth-looking skin is usually light tan with dark splotches, giving them almost a marbled look. House Geckos have slender tails, feet with adhesive toe pads that allow them to walk on walls, and eyes with no movable eyelids.

Behavior

House Geckos are nocturnal and so are most active at dusk and in the evening. They are also very vocal and like to call out in the evening.

You might find a House Gecko in a vertical hiding place because the species is arboreal and likes to climb.

Like other species of geckos, male House Geckos are territorial and so must be kept in separate enclosures. Females can be housed together, however, as can several females and one male.

81

Care

Because House Geckos like to climb, they should be kept in vertically oriented terrariums. A 10-gallon tank should suffice for one House Gecko, although your pet will be more comfortable if it has a larger space.

Bark is the best substrate for House Geckos. Place a few rocks in the terrarium for the gecko to climb on, along with several potted plants that like moist environments. Additionally, provide hiding places within the plants or in upright pieces of driftwood for the gecko to climb on and sleep in.

A heat source will be necessary since the House Gecko requires a daytime temperature of 82° to 90°F, with 69° to 72°F at night. Humidity is important for this tropical species, and should be kept at 70 to 90 percent. You can accomplish this by misting the gecko's tank once daily and providing a shallow water dish.

Feed your House Gecko crickets, spiders and other small insects. It will enjoy an occasional mealworm too. Periodically dust the insects with a vitamin and mineral powder before feeding.

Day Geckos

PHELSUMA SPECIES

There are approximately sixty different species of Day Geckos that fall under the *Phelsuma* genus. The species have similar natural histories and require similar care, so they are often grouped together for discussion. Some of the easier Day Geckos to care for are the Giant Madagascar Day Gecko *(Phelsuma madagascariensis grandis)*, the Gold Dust Gecko *(Phelsuma laticauda)* and Lined Day Gecko *(Phelsuma lineata)*.

Origins

Day Geckos first developed on the island of Madagascar, located off the eastern coast of Africa in the Indian Ocean. They still exist there in the wild, as well as on surrounding islands. Members of the *Gekkoninae* subfamily, Day Geckos have become very popular among reptile keepers. The success breeders have had in reproducing these geckos in captivity should begin to help ease the strain on native populations.

Appearance

Day Geckos all share a similar coloration; most are green, with different amounts of blue, white and red patterns. These patterns take the form of spots, mottling or stripes depending on the species.

Giant Madagascar Day Gecko

Although coloration is similar from species to species, there is a wide variety of sizes among Day Geckos. Some Day Geckos are as small as 3 inches long, while others grow to be nearly a foot long.

Because this species is very active during daylight hours, their eyes differ significantly from nocturnal geckos. Instead of the cat-like slit seen in the pupils of other geckos, Day Geckos have dark round pupils that fill up nearly the entire eye. They do not have movable eyelids, but they do have adhesive toe pads that help them climb and cling to vertical objects.

Day Geckos have relatively slender tails and more streamlined heads and necks than other gecko species. They have a different look than their nocturnal cousins, one that is easily recognized by an educated eye.

Behavior

As their name suggests, Day Geckos spend much of their active time during daylight hours. They are busy at night, too, making them a very alert and interesting pet.

Day Geckos are excellent climbers and enjoy scaling vertical objects in their enclosures and clinging to them. When they feel nervous, Day Geckos will slip into a hiding place to wait for danger to pass.

Because they are quick and can climb with such ease, some of the smaller geckos are notorious for being able to escape their enclosures. Be careful when opening and closing your terrarium cover, and make sure the enclosure is safe and secure.

Male Day Geckos are very territorial and should be kept separate from one another. A male may live with as many as three female Day Geckos, but it's important for you to keep an eye on the whole gang to make sure everyone is getting along peacefully.

Care

Because Day Geckos are such great climbers, they need a tall, vertically designed enclosure. The size of the terrarium depends on the size of the species. A small Day Gecko can do well in a 10-gallon tank, whereas a pair needs at least a 15-gallon enclosure. Individuals of the medium-sized species can live alone in a 25- to 30-gallon tank, and the giant Day Geckos need an even bigger enclosure. Some keepers in tropical climates maintain their giant Day Geckos in outdoor enclosures.

Good substrate for a Day Gecko consists of a half-inch layer of small pebbles covered with an inch or two of potting soil or orchid bark. (Make sure there is no Styrolite™ added to the potting soil.)

Put a number of tall-growing, big, hard-leafed tropical plants in your Day Gecko's terrarium. This lizard also enjoys climbing on bamboo stalks and using them as a resting or basking place in its enclosure. (Stand the stalks up vertically and diagonally.) The plants will also help keep the humidity level high.

Make sure the plant leaves provide good hiding places for your gecko. It will use these spots to sleep and to relieve stress when something frightens it.

Unlike nocturnal geckos, Day Geckos need full-spectrum lighting to maintain their health. The light will also help maintain your plants. Depending on the size of your terrarium, one or more full-spectrum lights should be placed on the top. Make sure the light shines through a screen top and not through glass, as the glass can impede the necessary UV light from reaching your gecko.

Basking is important to Day Geckos, so an incandescent bulb of anywhere from 40 to 60 watts or a halogen basking light should be provided. Place the light on one side of the cage, and make sure there is a spot underneath it where the gecko can lay to soak up the light.

Provide your Day Gecko with 14 hours a day of both incandescent and full-spectrum light during the summer and around 10 hours a day in the wintertime.

As you may have guessed, because this lizard hails from a tropical climate, the temperature in a Day Gecko's terrarium needs to be warm. The majority of Day Gecko species need daytime warmth of 82° to 89°F. At night, this can be reduced to 71° to 80°F. In the winter, reduce the daytime and nighttime temperatures by a few degrees.

Humidity is important for most Day Geckos. Keep your Day Gecko's terrarium at a relative humidity of 50 to 85 percent. Do this by spraying the inside of the tank with water a few times a day. (The exceptions to the rule are the Day Geckos that hail from the southwestern portion of Madagascar, such as the Drab Day Gecko. These lizards prefer a dryer climate.)

Day Geckos will drink from a shallow water dish, so one should be provided within the enclosure. This will help maintain the enclosure's humidity level as well.

Day Geckos enjoy eating crickets, locusts, grasshoppers, beetles, spiders and other small insects. These insects should be dusted with a vitamin and mineral supplement every other feeding.

Unlike other geckos that are strictly insectivores, Day Geckos will also feed on fruit and nectar. You can offer your Day Gecko mashed bananas, papaya or mango, a dampened sugar cube, or honey mixed with water.

Fan-Fingered Gecko
PTYODACTYLUS HASSELQUISTI

Also known as the Fat-Toed Gecko, this lizard's unique appearance makes it a favorite among hobbyists.

Origins

Members of the *Gekkoninae* subfamily, Fan-Fingered Geckos naturally live in the desert regions of northern Africa, particularly the Sahara Desert. There is also a possibility that this species may be breeding in the wild in Florida, due to escaped captive lizards. These geckos are sometimes available to hobbyists as pets but are usually wild-caught specimens.

Fan-Fingered Gecko

Appearance

This species is best known for its unusual toe pads. Adhesive and shaped like little fans, each toe tip spreads out, giving this gecko's feet the appearance of a star or snowflake.

The coloring of the Fan-Fingered Gecko is rather subtle. A light-brown base color is often topped off with white and darker brown spots or splotches. Some members of this species have no markings at all. The golden eyes are prominent and lack movable lids.

The body of the Fan-Fingered Gecko is somewhat flat looking. The head is large, and the lizard's limbs make it look a bit gangly. From head to tail, the Fan-Fingered Gecko grows to be around 6 inches long.

Behavior

Unlike other geckos, the Fan-Fingered Gecko is active at different times of the day. In its native land, it lives in rocky areas, where it does a lot of climbing. Its adhesive laminae enable it to cling to steep surfaces.

Male Fan-Fingered Geckos are rather vocal and make a loud clicking sound. They are territorial and should only be housed alone or with one or two females.

Care

Fan-Fingered Geckos like to climb, and this should be reflected in the enclosure you provide for your pet. A terrarium that is vertically designed is best. A single specimen can live comfortably in a 15-gallon enclosure, although a pair needs to be housed in a larger tank.

Fine sand makes an appropriate substrate for Fan-Fingered Geckos. A collection of rocks should be provided for the lizards to climb on. The rocks can be real or artificial. If they are real, be sure to securely glue them together so they don't accidentally fall on your pet and injure it.

Provide your Fan-Fingered Gecko with a heat source. The terrarium should be kept warm, with an area where the lizard can bask. An incandescent light can provide this warmth during the day. Cool the tank down to 75°F or so at night. Also provide a shallow water dish for your pet to drink from.

Fan-Fingered Geckos can be fed a variety of insects from a pesticide-free yard. These include beetles, grasshoppers and spiders. You can also give them commercially bred crickets and mealworms dusted with a vitamin and mineral supplement.

Wall Gecko

TARENTOLA MAURITANICA

The Wall Gecko is a commonly available gecko, and is also known by the common names of Moorish Gecko, Mauritanian Gecko and Crocodile Gecko. Individuals are bred in captivity on a regular basis, although imports are still commonly sold.

Origins

This gecko is a member of the *Gekkoninae* subfamily. It originated on the Mediterranean coast and has since spread to the Canary Islands, parts of Greece and northern Africa. It is commonly seen living on the rooftops of buildings in European cities.

Appearance

The Wall Gecko grows to a length of no more than around 6 inches. It has a chunky body type and a large head. There are rough, sharp-looking scales over its neck, legs, back and tail, giving a crocodile-type look (hence one of its many common names).

The Wall Gecko tends to be a rather dull gray or brown with splotches of lighter color. Its eyes are an amber shade with distinct vertical slits in the daylight. It does not have movable eyelids.

The Wall Gecko has distinctive toe pads that help it hold onto vertical surfaces. Unlike other geckos that have claws on each toe, only the Wall Gecko's third and fourth toes contain a claw.

Behavior

The Wall Gecko is primarily nocturnal, although it is somewhat active during the day when the temperature is cooler.

This climbing gecko enjoys scaling the sides of walls and buildings in the wild, and climbing on rocks and other surfaces in captivity.

Wall Geckos tend to move slowly around their terrarium, but if you attempt to catch one, it can quickly dart away. While this species doesn't normally vocalize, it will cry out if captured.

Male Wall Geckos are territorial and should be maintained one per enclosure or with only one female.

Care

Wall Geckos are relatively easy to care for. Because they like to climb, they should be housed in a large vertical terrarium of at least 20 gallons for one specimen. A 25- to 30-gallon terrarium will be necessary for a pair.

Substrate for this species can be sand or bark. Give your Wall Gecko some rocks to climb on, either real or artificial. Glue the rocks together and to the bottom of the terrarium so they don't accidentally fall on your pet and injure it.

A heat source will be needed to maintain this gecko in good health. Because these geckos also like to bask occasionally, providing an artificial light source is a good idea, especially if you intend to keep your lizard in an area of the house that doesn't get a lot of natural sunlight. Keep the terrarium at around 80°F during the day, and cool it off to about 77°F at night. Provide a mist spray of water each night to mimic the damper evenings of this gecko's native environment. If you live in a very dry climate, you may need to mist more often because this species' terrarium humidity should be kept around 50 percent.

Feed your Wall Gecko a variety of insects gathered from a pesticide-free yard. Commercially bred crickets and an occasional feeding of mealworms are suitable, although Wall Geckos thrive on a varied diet. Don't forget to dust the insects with a vitamin and mineral supplement twice a week.

Wonder Gecko

TERATOSCINCUS SCINCUS

The Wonder Gecko is an unusual-looking species that is somewhat difficult for newcomers to the hobby to keep. It is one of several members of the *Teratoscincus* genus.

Origins

The natural range of the Wonder Gecko includes all of eastern Arabia—including the northern regions of Iran and Afghanistan and along the Caspian sea—as well as the western part of China. It is a member of the *Gekkoninae* subfamily.

Appearance

Small Scaled Wonder Gecko or Dwarf Frog-Eyed Gecko

The Wonder Gecko's appearance makes it an often desired specimen among gecko keepers. Its body is covered with plate-like scales on a pale yellow background. There are gray, brown, and black marble and patchwork patterns all over its body. Individuals with a light blue background color are also seen on occasion.

The Wonder Gecko's body is stocky, supporting a rather large head. It has strong arms and legs, and claws on its feet to help it dig. This gecko has interesting, lidless eyes that are kaleidoscope-patterned and dark green in color. Because they resemble a frogs eyes to many, the common name Frog-Eyed Gecko is sometimes used to describe this species.

BEHAVIOR

Since this species originates in a dry, desert-like environment, nature equipped it with the ability to dig its own burrows to escape the heat of the sun. Wonder Geckos like to create their own hiding places.

Wonder Geckos use sound to protect their territory. They utter a distinct call when warning other geckos to move out of range. They also make a loud scraping noise by rubbing the scales on their tail together.

It's not easy to pin these lizards down to a particular time of day. They are known to be nocturnal, but they are also active at dawn and dusk.

Males of the species are territorial and should be kept apart. When males are in close proximity of each other, they will fight. If frightened, Wall Geckos display a defensive posture resembling that of a frightened cat. They stand up tall, arch their backs, swish their tails, open their mouths wide and expand their throats.

CARE

Wonder Geckos need a lot of space to roam, even in captivity. Provide a single specimen with a 20-gallon or larger terrarium.

Sand mixed with loam is a good substrate for these desert dwellers. Because Wonder Geckos spend much of their time in moist burrows in the wild, it's important to provide them with just the right subterranean environment. Some experts recommend at least 8 inches of substrate to allow the gecko to dig. The bottom layers should be kept moistened. This can be done by keeping several rocks at one end of the terrarium, making sure they reach all the way to the bottom of the tank. Pour a small amount of water on the rocks every so often so the water will run down the bottom layer of substrate. The goal is to moisten, but not saturate, the environment. It can be tricky to maintain the right amount of moisture in this way, but practice makes perfect.

The temperature in your Wonder Gecko's terrarium should be 85° to 90°F during the day. Provide one section of the enclosure with more heat, using a heat pad or overhead light. Lower the overall temperature at night to 70°F.

Wonder Geckos also need a winter cooling session of about eight weeks when the terrarium temperature should be brought down to around 60°F during the day.

It's important to feed Wonder Geckos a wide variety of insects, particularly beetles. They can also be fed commercially bred crickets and mealworms. Dust the food with vitamin and mineral supplement ever other feeding. Provide water in a shallow dish.

Flat-Tailed Gecko
UROPLATUS FIMBRIATUS
This unusual-looking gecko has become increasingly popular with herp keepers. There was a time when only imported wild-caught individuals were available, but specimens are now being bred in captivity.

Origins
The Flat-Tailed Gecko is native to the rain forests of Madagascar and nearby islands. It is a member of the *Gekkoninae* subfamily and is sold in both America and Europe.

Appearance
This species is a most unusual-looking creature. As its name suggests, it has a tail that looks like it was run over by a steamroller. By contrast, its body is somewhat round and its head rather long and angular. The Flat-Tailed Gecko has adhesive toe pads on large, flat feet. Growing to be as big as 8 inches long, the Flat-Tailed Gecko is a pebbly brown color with a green or sometimes yellow hue.

The edges of the Flat-Tailed Gecko's body are serrated in appearance, helping it blend in against the wood of a tree or a blanket of leaves where, in nature, it would lie in wait for its prey. It also has huge, amber or yellow-colored eyes with vertical slits when viewed in the light. It does not have movable eyelids.

Behavior

Flat-Tailed Geckos are nocturnal and somewhat inactive. Rather than seeking out their prey, they tend to wait for insects to amble by. They then pounce on them with great force.

During the day, Flat-Tailed Geckos prefer to hide under something and sleep. However, they come to life at night and are best viewed at this time.

Male Flat-Tailed Geckos are territorial and should not be kept together lest they fight with one another.

Care

To successfully keep a Flat-Tailed Gecko, you need to recreate its rain-forest environment. Start with a vertically designed terrarium at least 3 feet high and 2 feet wide.

Phantastic Flat-Tailed Gecko

A combination of orchid bark and peat moss makes a good substrate for this species. The substrate should be misted daily. Provide potted, leafy tropical plants in the enclosure too. This will give your Flat-Tailed Gecko something to climb on and will help increase the humidity in the tank. Pieces of cork bark will also give your pet someplace to hide during the day.

The temperature in your Flat-Tailed Gecko's enclosure should be between 68° and 78°F during the day and a few degrees cooler in the evening. It's especially important to make sure the temperature does not go above 80°F for any extended period of time, as this can ultimately shorten a Flat-Tailed Gecko's life.

Flat-Tailed Geckos enjoy a variety of insects from a pesticide-free yard. You can also give them commercially bred crickets and an occasional feeding of mealworms. Cockroaches are a particular favorite of Flat-Tailed Geckos. Be sure to dust all insects with vitamin and mineral supplement every other feeding. A shallow dish filled with water should always be available.

Yellow-Headed Gecko
GONATODES ALBOGULARIS FUSCUS

There are several subspecies of this gecko, but *Gonatodes albogularis fuscus* is one of the better-known geckos among reptile keepers. This interesting lizard makes a good pet and is readily available in the pet trade. It is also known by the common name White-Throated Gecko.

Origins

The Yellow-Headed Gecko is found naturally in the northern region of South America and in Central America and the West Indies. Escaped captives have populated certain areas of Florida, including the Keys. They spend time in wilderness regions as well as in farmland and developed areas. The Yellow-Headed Gecko is a member of the *Sphaerodactylinae* subfamily.

Appearance

The Yellow-Headed Gecko is one of the smaller species of gecko, measuring in at about 4 inches long in adulthood. It has a thick body and a strong head, with substantial limbs. The Yellow-Headed Gecko's toes, which lack adhesive pads, are exceptionally long.

This species gets its name from the coloration of the male. From the neck to the tip of the tail, the Yellow-Headed Gecko can be light brown, dark brown, gray or nearly black. The color of the gecko's head ranges from yellow to bright orange.

Female Yellow-Headed Geckos, on the other hand, tend to be light brown or gray with darker and lighter mottling. Their throats usually show a light band.

The lidless eyes of the Yellow-Headed Gecko have round pupils, like those of Day Geckos.

Behavior

Yellow-Headed Geckos are diurnal, which means they are most active during the day.

Despite the fact that they lack adhesive toe pads, Yellow-Headed Geckos enjoy hanging on the underside of tree limbs. They will do this in captivity too if provided the right environment.

The males of the species are territorial and should only be housed alone or with one female.

Madagascar Yellow-Headed Day Gecko

Care

A 10-gallon horizontal terrarium is adequate for one or two Yellow-Headed Geckos, although they will enjoy the largest tank that you can provide.

Good substrates for this species include reptile sand or bark. Because Yellow-Headed Geckos enjoy climbing and hanging on tree limbs, horizontally placed branches will be appreciated by your pet.

The temperature in your Yellow-Headed Gecko's terrarium should be about 84°F during the day, and a bit lower at night. You should provide full-spectrum lighting, along with humidity at about 50 percent by spraying the tank with water every day. A potted plant or two in the terrarium will help maintain a high humidity level.

Yellow-Headed Geckos will eat many different insects and should be offered some variety. Spiders, beetles and other insects from a pesticide-free garden will be appreciated, in addition to commercially bred crickets and sparse feedings of mealworms. Be sure to dust the insects with vitamin and mineral supplement at every other feeding. Provide water in a shallow dish at all times.

Reef Gecko

SPHAERODACTYLUS NOTATUS

The Reef Gecko, a United States native, is easy to find and to care for.

Origins

A member of the *Sphaerodactylinae* subfamily, the Reef Gecko is native to Florida and the West Indies. It can be seen quite commonly around inhabited areas of Florida, particularly near water.

Appearance

Reef Geckos are very tiny creatures, measuring only around 2½ inches long. They have thin bodies and limbs, a pointed nose and no movable eyelids. The tail is long and narrow. Their toe pads are adhesive, enabling them to climb and hold on with great skill.

This species does not display particularly spectacular colors and can best be described as simply a pale brown. There are some lighter and darker markings that connect together to form stripes on the sides of the head, but overall, they are not remarkable. The tail can be a somewhat slightly orange-brown color.

Behavior

Reef Geckos are most active during the day and at dawn and dusk, although they prefer to stay under cover even when hunting. They enjoy spending time on the ground in areas where there are leaves and other debris for them to hide in. They also hide out under the peeling bark of trees.

Reef Geckos are known for being able to move very quickly and can dart away from a handler at lightening speed.

Males are territorial and should be kept alone in an enclosure or with a female only.

Care

You should house your single Reef Gecko or pair of geckos in a 15-gallon or larger terrarium. A horizontal design is best because these geckos are primarily terrestrial.

Reef Geckos do best in a substrate made up of sand, peat moss and some leaves. The leaves are important because they will give your pet someplace to hide out. A piece of wood and a potted plant will also help provide a natural habitat for it.

Proper heat is crucial for this tropical lizard and should be maintained at around 85°F during the day and around 70°F at night. Because these lizards are diurnal, they need full-spectrum lighting. An additional heat source will be necessary for the evenings if you live in a cool climate.

> **KEY FACTORS IN CHOOSING A LIZARD**
>
> • How much space are you willing to devote to your lizard's cage?
>
> • If you will have more than one lizard, do you have room to house them separately, if necessary?
>
> • Will you be willing to feed your lizard insects?
>
> • Will your children and other family members be willing to learn how to properly care for a delicate lizard?

You will need to provide a humid environment for your Reef Gecko, of anywhere from 50 to 80 percent. Spray the inside of the terrarium daily with a mist of water, and provide at least one plant to help maintain moisture in the air.

Because Reef Geckos are so tiny, they need especially small insects to eat, such as termites, aphids, houseflies, pinhead crickets and small spiders. Dust these insects with a vitamin and mineral supplement at every other feeding. Remember to provide a shallow dish for fresh water.

White-Lined Gecko
GEKKO VITTATUS

The White-Lined Gecko, also known as the Indonesian Skunk Gecko, has not been widely available to hobbyists until recently.

Origins
The White-Lined Gecko is native to Oceania and Indonesia, where it lives in a savanna-type environment in the wild. It is a member of the *Gekkoninae* subfamily.

Appearance
This species of gecko has a most unusual appearance. Its base color is yellowish brown, and in most individuals there is a white stripe that begins alongside the gecko's ear and extends just past the base of the tail, ending in a triangular shape.

Although the White-Lined Gecko is named for this marking, it does not appear on every individual within the species. Instead, some patches of white or light color will be seen along the lizard's backbone.

The body of the White-Lined Gecko is long and lean, and can grow to 8 inches in length. This gecko has lidless, amber-colored eyes with a prong above each one. There are adhesive toe pads on each clawed foot.

Behavior
These lizards are nocturnal creatures and are very active during the evening hours, when they do all their hunting.

Being hardy climbers, White-Lined Geckos also enjoy being high up off the ground and lounging in trees and plants.

They are highly territorial geckos and should be kept in only very small groups. Males can live only with one other female, and never with one another.

Care

Because White-Lined Geckos are so active, a single specimen or pair does best in a 20-gallon or larger vertically shaped terrarium.

The substrate for a White-Lined Gecko enclosure should be a mixture of sand and peat moss. Rocks of different sizes should be in-cluded too, along with branches, corkwood and other materials. Give your White-Lined Gecko plenty of tall objects for climbing and hiding.

Maintain your White-Lined Gecko's terrarium at around 85°F during the day and a little lower at night. Since these lizards are nocturnal, there's no need for full-spectrum lighting. Your pet's enclosure should be misted with water once a day to maintain proper humidity.

White-Striped Gecko

Feed your White-Lined Gecko a variety of small insects, dusted with a vitamin and mineral supplement. A shallow dish filled with water should be kept in the terrarium.

Kuhl's Flying Gecko
PTYCHOZOON KUHLII

Of the five different species of Flying Geckos, the most commonly kept is *Ptychozoon kuhlii*. All Flying Geckos can be difficult to keep and are best for experienced herpetoculturists, although they are being bred successfully in captivity.

Origins

Kuhl's Flying Gecko hails from Malaysia and nearby islands, where it lives in the tropical rain forest. Flying Geckos are members of the *Gekkoninae* subfamily.

Appearance

This gecko, reaching an adult length of 8 inches, is rather uninteresting in terms of its color. Its body features a dull brown color with sporadic splotches of gray and a darker brown.

Kuhl's Flying Gecko more than makes up for its appearance with its unique and intriguing body type. It has a loose flap of skin on both sides of its body, which begins behind the front limbs and extends all the way to the back legs. It also has adhesive toe pads on very webbed feet, and its eyes are lidless and prominent.

Behavior

Flying Geckos have one behavioral characteristic that sets them apart from other geckos: They have the ability to "fly" short distances, using their skin flaps as sails.

Flying Gecko

The primary purpose for this is to enable the gecko to move from higher branches to lower branches without injuring itself. This special skin also aids the lizard in camouflaging itself.

These fascinating geckos are nocturnal and do their hunting and "flying" at night. They are also territorial, and males should be kept apart or with a single female.

Care

Kuhl's Flying Geckos require tall, vertical terrariums in order to feel at home. The enclosure should be at least a 15-gallon tank or larger.

Provide a substrate of peat moss or bark, and place several heavy branches in the tank. You should consider keeping some leafy, tropical plants in the enclosure too. This will help maintain the humidity and give your gecko additional privacy, as these geckos like to hide during the day. You may want to consider adding a piece of cork wood since some individuals in this species will hide on the ground.

Heat is important to this tropical dweller, so include some kind of heat source for the enclosure, keeping the temperature at around 83°F during the day and 73°F at night. Because it is nocturnal, Kuhl's Flying Gecko does not need full-spectrum lighting. However, you can provide an incandescent light during the day to help the plants in the terrarium. If this is your primary heat source, use a red light at night so your gecko will come out to hunt.

It is necessary to maintain a high humidity level in a Kuhl's Flying Gecko's environment. Spray the inside of the terrarium several times a day to keep it moist.

Feed different insects to your pet in addition to commercially bred crickets and occasional mealworms. Spiders, small grasshoppers and cockroaches are appreciated. Be sure to coat them with a vitamin and mineral supplement before every other serving.

Your Kuhl's Flying Gecko will probably get its water from the droplets that form on the leaves you are spraying each day, but it's good to provide a shallow water dish should it need additional water.

Wahlberg's Velvet Gecko
HOMOPHOLIS WAHLBERGI
This interesting gecko is popular with hobbyists because of its unusual markings. It is not always readily available, however, and most specimens are imported.

Origins
A member of the *Gekkoninae* subfamily, Wahlberg's Velvet Gecko makes its natural home in South Africa. There it lives not only in semi-arid regions, but also near rivers where the air is more humid.

Appearance
Wahlberg's Velvet Gecko grows to about 8 inches long. It's body is stocky, and it has short toes with adhesive

pads. The eyes of Wahlberg's Velvet Gecko are lidless and amber in color.

This lizard is well-known for its coloration. The background color varies from gray to light brown. Thick black or dark-brown stripes run the length of its body, from behind the gecko's eyes all the way to the base of its tail. Down the center of its back, between the lines, are lighter patches, equally spaced apart. The markings turns into crossbands on the tail, with alternating dark and light colors.

Behavior

Wahlberg's Velvet Gecko is nocturnal, spending most of its active hunting time at night. During the day, it

Wahlberg's Velvet Gecko

hides in rock crevices. Because it is terrestrial, this species spends all of its time on the ground. While it can climb and adhere to rocks and other surfaces, it is not a tree dweller.

Whalberg's Velvet Geckos are territorial, and males should not be kept together.

Care

A 20- or 30-gallon horizontal terrarium is best for one or two of these lizards. Use sand or small gravel as a substrate, with some potted arid-climate plants. Because the Wahlberg's Velvet Gecko feels most at home climbing on rocks, be sure to provide some piles where it can hide and forage. Glue the rocks together so they won't fall down and injure your pet.

The temperature in your Wahlberg's Velvet Gecko's terrarium doesn't need to be too warm. A range of 78° to 82°F during the day is fine, provided by a heat pad or incandescent light. Bring this temperature down a few degrees at night.

This species doesn't need a lot of humidity, but an occasional spritz of water inside the terrarium will help the gecko shed. There's no need for full-spectrum lighting either, although you should provide incandescent light as a substitute for daylight if there's little natural light near your pet's terrarium.

Wahlberg's Velvet Gecko will eat a variety of insects, such as crickets, grasshoppers, spiders, beetles and an occasional mealworm. Dust the insects with a vitamin and mineral supplement before every other meal. Keep a shallow dish filled with water inside the terrarium too.

Four-Clawed Gecko
GEHYRA MUTILATA

A simple and accessible lizard, the Four-Clawed Gecko is growing in popularity with reptile keepers.

Origins
The Four-Clawed Gecko is native to Southeast Asia and a variety of Pacific Islands. A member of the *Gekkoninae* subfamily, it has been introduced to Hawaii. It is also known by the common name of the Pacific Gecko.

Appearance
As its name suggests, this gecko has only four claws instead of the usual five. (The claw is missing from the inside toe of each foot.) However, all five toes have adhesive pads.

The Four-Clawed Gecko has a smooth, stocky body, a large angular head and a lean tail. The small scales give its delicate skin a flat, uniform look. This species grows to be approximately 5 inches long.

Coloration in the species runs from gray to tan with no markings on its body. Its eyes are large and lidless.

Behavior
The Four-Clawed Gecko is nocturnal and does its hunting and moving around mostly at night. During the day, it prefers to hide between rocks or under pieces of driftwood. The Four-Clawed Gecko is a rather vocal

gecko, and known for making chirping calls during the night. The males are territorial, and so should be housed alone or with only one or two females.

Care

A 15-gallon terrarium is adequate for housing one or two Four-Clawed Geckos. A horizontally oriented enclosure is best for this terrestrial lizard. A good substrate for it is orchid bark. Your pet will also appreciate a tropical plant or two, plus a hiding place made from wood or rocks that have been glued together to ensure they don't collapse on the tenant.

The Four-Clawed Gecko needs a warm environment, with temperatures ranging from 78° to 82°F. In the evening, the temperature can drop a few degrees. Use a heat pad or an incandescent light to provide warmth for your pet. It also needs humidity of at least 60 percent, which can be achieved with a daily misting of water inside the terrarium. Plants can help maintain the right level of humidity.

Feed your Four-Clawed Gecko on a variety of small insects, including crickets, mealworms, spiders, sow bugs and cockroaches, dusted with a vitamin and mineral supplement. It will also eat small bits of over-ripe fruit. Don't forget to provide a shallow dish for water. Not only can your gecko drink from this if it wishes, it will also help maintain the appropriate humidity in your terrarium.

Thick-Tailed Gecko

UNDERWOODISAURUS MILI

A rather uncommon lizard in captivity, the Thick-Tailed Gecko is renowned for its unusual appearance.

Origins

A member of the *Diplodactyliniae* subfamily, the Thick-Tailed Gecko originated in the south of Australia.

Appearance

Unlike most other gecko species, the Thick-Tailed Gecko has a very dark, almost mahogany body color.

There are off-white spotted patterns across its head, back and legs. The tail has distinct crossbands.

Growing to 5 inches long in adulthood, the Thick-Tailed Gecko has a big head for its body. Its limbs are rather spindly in appearance, and its tail is somewhat short. It has adhesive toe pads and large eyes with no movable lids.

Behavior

In addition to its unique appearance, the Thick-Tailed Gecko has some unusual behaviors. It has a defensive posture that includes standing on its back legs and leaping forward at whatever is threatening it. A loud vocalization may also be made at the same time.

This lizard from "Down Under" is nocturnal and prefers to stay close to the ground. It hides during the day and hunts at night by lurking through leaves and other ground matter.

Males of the species are territorial and should be kept apart. A male can be housed safely with a single female.

Care

A Thick-Tailed Gecko is most comfortable in a 15- to 20-gallon, horizontal terrarium. Provide a substrate that combines bark and leaves, or sand and peat moss, with leaves strewn on top. Your pet will hide under the leaves during the day, as well as in a piece of cork wood that you provide.

The best temperature range for a Thick-Tailed Gecko terrarium is 81° to 83°F during the day and in the high 60s at night. The heat source can be a heat pad or incandescent light. Some humidity is required, and can be achieved by misting the interior of the terrarium with water daily.

Your Thick-Tailed Gecko eats small insects, including crickets, spiders, sow bugs and cockroaches. It will also enjoy an occasional mealworm. At least twice a week, be sure to dust its food with a vitamin and mineral supplement before feeding. A shallow water dish should also be provided.

Texas Banded Gecko
COLEONYX BREVIS

This native American species is easy to keep and is closely related to the Banded Gecko.

Origins
Areas of northern Mexico and the Rio Grande Valley in Texas are home to this member of the *Eublepharinae*

Texas Banded Gecko

subfamily. Its existence was discovered in the 1950s.

Appearance
One of the smaller geckos, the Texas Banded measures around 4 to 5 inches long. The males are generally larger than the females. Its coloration is similar to that of the Leopard Gecko, although it has a leaner body type as well as a longer head and neck.

The Texas Banded Gecko has a pale yellow or cream-colored body with dark-brown spots. Faint, pale bands can be seen underneath the spots, which are left over from the lizard's juvenile coat pattern. The Texas Banded Gecko has eyelids that open and close much like our own do. Its feet have tiny claws but no adhesive toe pads.

Behavior
A nocturnal lizard, the Texas Banded Gecko prefers to hide and sleep during the day. In the wild, it spends

much of its waking time on rocks waiting for insects to happen by.

Males of this species are territorial and must be housed separately. A male and one or two females can be kept together in one terrarium.

Care

House your Texas Banded Gecko in a 10-gallon or larger horizontal terrarium. If you plan to keep more than one of these geckos together, use a larger enclosure.

Texas Banded Geckos do well on a fine sand substrate, orchid bark or even reptile carpet. They need a secure place to hide during the day, either a crevice constructed with rocks securely glued together, or a wood hideout. You can even add a real or artificial desert plant, although spiny cactus are not recommended, as they can injure your pet.

> ### CREATIVE ESCAPE
>
> The Texas Banded Gecko can sever its tail to distract a perceived threat. The portion of tail that is left behind wiggles and squirms to distract a predator, while the owner gets away and eventually grows another tail.

Keep your Texas Banded Gecko warm during the day at about 86° and 77°F at night. Use a heat pad or incandescent light to warm the enclosure. If you opt for the light as a heat source, be sure to use only a red bulb at night so as not to disturb your gecko's internal clock.

Not much humidity is required by this species. When your pet starts shedding, spray a mist of water near its hiding place to help it shed its skin. Other than this, no other misting is required.

Texas Banded Geckos eat a variety of small insects. Commercially bred crickets are fine for them as long as they are dusted several times a week before being given to your pet. Keep a shallow dish of drinking water in your gecko's enclosure.

chapter 8

Gecko

Behavior

One of the best things about owning a gecko is observing its behavior. Geckos are interesting creatures and can provide you with hours of observational enjoyment.

Hunting

Geckos are excellent hunters and are entertaining to watch.

Pay attention to your gecko the next time you feed it. Geckos are opportunistic feeders and won't deliberately go searching for prey. But if an unsuspecting insect comes within their field of vision, watch out! Geckos rarely miss their prey.

If your gecko is feeling hungry and it spies an insect, it will begin to stalk the insect much like a cat would stalk a mouse. It will move with a very deliberate and stilted motion, all the while focusing intently on its victim. Once it gets within striking distance, the gecko will take a second to get the insect directly "within its crosshairs," and then, in the blink of an eye, the insect will be inside the gecko's mouth. Sometimes, just before the gecko strikes, its tail begins to quiver intensely.

The next step in the process is to swallow the insect, which the gecko does with merely a few movements of its head. Many geckos will then lick their lips almost as if to say "Wow, that was good."

Crickets are a nutritious meal and make good prey for a hungry gecko. (Uroplatus sikorae)

Shedding

Another one of the gecko's interesting behaviors comes when it's time for the lizard to shed its skin. Just prior to molting, many geckos become less active. Then, as the skin begins to separate from the lizard's body, the gecko will try to help it along by pulling at it and swallowing it whole. Geckos can often be seen trying to pull the most stubborn pieces off their toes, much like a dog would try to chew a burr out of its fur.

Territoriality

Geckos, particularly males, are notorious for being territorial. In fact, male geckos will fight violently to protect their turf. The gecko prefaces an attack by threatening his foe with a bobbing of his head.

The main motivation behind this territoriality lies in the gecko's mating instinct. By protecting his territory, a male gecko is also protecting his right to breed with any females that are within the area. In captivity, male geckos will fight whether or not a female is present— the instinct is still there.

Female geckos occasionally become territorial as well, driven by an instinct to protect their nests and have access to the greatest food supply.

Mating

Most novice gecko owners are not ready to take on the hobby of breeding their geckos, since this can be a time-consuming and complicated task. However, it is interesting to note some of the different behavioral patterns that relate to gecko courtship.

> ### SOME GECKOS ARE CLONES
>
> Oddly enough, some gecko species are parthenogenetic, which means that the females can reproduce without a male partner. In these situations, the resulting offspring are actually genetic clones of the female. It is surmised that nature created this condition in order to help the species survive during times when the gecko population is low and mates are few and far between.

When male and female geckos are introduced, the male will usually vocalize to her, making whatever sounds are inherent to his species. A circling ritual will also ensue, along with some head bobbing and tail writhing. This is the way male and female geckos "get acquainted," and a mating usually results soon after. Scientists also believe that this courtship might be instrumental in inducing ovulation in the female gecko.

Nesting

Female geckos are not devout mothers like female mammals are, but they are more nurturing than many other reptiles. When a female is close to egg-laying time, she will select a secure place to deposit the eggs. The arboreal species tend to glue their eggs high up so they hang vertically. Terrestrial species lay their eggs on the ground, usually in a secure spot rich in substrate.

The females of some gecko species will actually protect their eggs, fighting with other geckos that get too close to the nest. In fact, both the male and female Tokay Gecko will guard the eggs and show aggression to any other lizard that nears the nest. Female Tokay Geckos have been known to cannibalize the eggs of other females, which explains this defensive behavior.

Terrestrial geckos usually lay their eggs in a safe area on the ground. This Leopard Gecko is emerging from its egg.

Hiding

Although hiding isn't exactly one of the most fascinating gecko behaviors to watch, it is nonetheless an important activity for the gecko. Nature has equipped geckos with the instinct to take cover when they are sleeping so predators won't make a meal out of them when they are most vulnerable.

Different species of geckos prefer to hide in different ways. Arboreal species, like the Tokay Gecko, prefer to tuck their bodies behind leaves and under peeling bark. Some terrestrial species, like the Thick Tailed Gecko, prefer to hide on the ground under leaf litter. Other terrestrial geckos, like the Leopard Gecko, are happy to stash their bodies away beneath a piece of wood or rock.

Hiding is such an important behavior in geckos that any gecko which isn't provided a hiding place can become so stressed it will get sick and die.

The Gecko Personality

Although geckos don't have the same kind of behavioral traits as mammals, they do nonetheless have distinctive personalities. Indeed, different species are inclined toward different kinds of temperaments. While Leopard Geckos tend to be quiet and easygoing, Tokays are aggressive and hard to handle. Banded Geckos prefer to hide all day under a rock or piece of wood, while Day Geckos want to be out in the sunshine, watching the world go by.

By taking the time to spend quietly watching your gecko, you'll discover its unique personality.

Gecko personalities are not only unique to their species, but also to each individual lizard. Anyone who has spent any quality time around geckos will agree with this observation.

Geckos are fascinating to watch, not only because they are beautiful, but also because they have real personality. The best way to discover your particular gecko's distinct personality is to quietly observe it. Keep its terrarium in a place that is relatively peaceful yet where you spend enough time so as to notice its activities.

If you watch your pet closely, you'll discover all kinds of things about its personality. You will probably see that it has certain preferences when it comes to food. Your gecko may look nonchalantly at crickets and only hunt them when it's really hungry, but pounce on mealworms the instant you place them in its enclosure.

You may also notice that your particular gecko likes to perch in a certain spot in its terrarium, looking down over its enclosure like a king observing its domain. Or, it could be the type that prefers to lie around underneath its hiding place or an overhanging leaf rather than take in the big picture.

If you have more than one gecko of the same species, you will clearly see differences in each individual. Every gecko is a unique being, with its own special preferences and characteristics. One of the most interesting and fun aspects of gecko ownership is discovering the particular nuances of your individual pet.

The Outside World

You may think your gecko's world is limited only to what is going on inside its terrarium, but this is not true. I discovered this first-hand one day shortly after acquiring Gordon, my Leopard Gecko. I had placed a white container of crickets on the floor near Gordon's terrarium, which is in my home office (a great place to keep your gecko's enclosure, by the way). As I sat at my computer working, I noticed that Gordon had come out of his hiding place and was standing with his nose up against the glass, staring intently in the direction of the cricket container. I glanced over at the container, wondering what he was looking at, and discovered that an army of tiny black ants had attacked my crickets! Thanks to Gordon's acute observation, I was able to rescue my crickets from a league of marauding ants.

You may not have had the chance to experience anything quite like this scene, but if you pay close attention, you'll notice that *your* gecko is aware of its outside surroundings, too. If you have the cause to ever move your pet's enclosure, you'll see plenty of evidence of your pet's observational abilities.

When you move your gecko's enclosure from one place to another, you will probably notice a significant increase in your pet's activity. If you have a nocturnal gecko that usually hides during the day, you'll see your pet come out of its hiding place and start exploring the edges of its terrarium with avid curiosity, looking out through the glass in an obvious attempt to figure out what's going on. It's also possible that your nocturnal gecko may become frightened by what is happening and will quickly sequester itself in its hiding place, refusing to come out until things have settled down.

If you have a diurnal gecko, it will also take note of the change in scenery. You'll see it looking around, noticing that its enclosure no longer has the same outside scenery as it did before. If it gets nervous, it may find itself a cozy leaf to hide under.

A nocturnal gecko, such as the popular Leopard Gecko, may respond to a change in its surroundings by spending more time than usual out and about in the daylight.

Even though the interior of its terrarium has stayed the same, this change in the outside world can be rather stressful for your pet. To help it adjust to its new surroundings, avoid handling it for several days before and after the move. You should also withhold food during that time because stress is particularly taxing for geckos with full stomachs. Let it settle in before you offer it food in its new home.

Note: Before you pick up your gecko's terrarium and move it elsewhere, remove the water dish and any other accessories that could injure your pet should they topple over and fall on him during the jostling that always occurs during a move.

Another example of your gecko's awareness to the outside world is how it reacts to other pets you may have.

If you have a cat or dog, and your pet likes to sit out-side your gecko's enclosure and watch it, your gecko will surely notice. If the dog or cat sits quietly and is not threatening, (and you have a particularly mellow gecko species), this can be an acceptable arrangement. However, if your cat or dog runs around, jumps on top of the terrarium or worse yet, tries to break into it, your gecko will be stressed by what is going on outside its home. Keep your cat or dog away from your gecko's terrarium if the animal does anything other than sit quietly and observe.

As you can see, your gecko is very sensitive to changes in its environment. For this reason, it's best to leave the accessories and dishes inside the terrarium in the same place. Geckos are creatures of habit and expect to find their hiding places, water dishes, and other cage acces-sories in the same place every day. "Redecorating" just for the sake of change may be fun for you, but it will be very stressful for your gecko!

Change of Seasons

Just about every creature on the planet notices when the seasons start to change. The seasons are part of the cycle of life, and even tiny insects are sensitive to them.

Your gecko is no exception to this rule. Geckos re-spond to the changes in temperature and light when in the wild, so it's only natural they should notice these things in captivity, too. In fact, people who breed geckos will create artificial winter and summer using con-trolled lighting to encourage their animals to breed.

Nocturnal geckos that have no source of artificial light in their terrariums are most likely to take notice when the sun begins to noticeably set earlier in the day dur-ing the fall or later in the day during the spring. Even though the pets are indoors and are provided with an artificial heat source, they also tend to be aware of the change in temperature from warm seasons to cool, and vice versa.

You can tell that your pet is responding to the change in seasons by observing its activity. Geckos tend to be

Geckos
Close-Up

more active in the warmer seasons than the cooler ones, so you may notice a difference in your pet when summer's heat turns to autumn cool. He may begin to eat a little bit less and spend less time moving around his enclosure. Although geckos don't hibernate, they do have a reduction in activity during the cooler months. Make sure you compensate for this change in weather by providing an adequate heat source for your pet.

You may also notice a behavior change in your gecko when winter turns to spring. Your lazy lizard may start coming out from its hiding space more often and be a little more interested in those crickets and mealworms now that the sun is staying in the sky a bit longer. Enjoy your pet's subtle reactions to the seasons while still providing it with the natural heat source it requires to stay healthy. Let it help you celebrate the changing seasons in its own, lizard-like fashion.

Home Alone

Because we humans are such social creatures, it can be hard for us to understand animals that do not need the interaction of their own kind. In the wild, geckos are solitary creatures that establish their own territory where they live, hunt, and breed. Male geckos will fight vehemently to defend this territory from other male geckos, and in fact some will not tolerate the presence of other geckos at all except during breeding time.

You may feel a bit uncomfortable with the idea of keeping your gecko all by itself in a terrarium because you may have the notion that the gecko is lonely. If your gecko had the psyche of a human being—or even a dog or cat—your notion would be correct. Most mammals thrive on the companionship of others, especially our domesticated friends.

Your gecko is a whole different critter, however. By providing it with a space that it can call its own, without other geckos to compete with for food or space, you are actually doing it a favor! Geckos prefer to be alone most of the time. It is less stressful for them, and

116

because stress can be damaging to a gecko's immune system, it is ultimately the healthiest way to keep them.

A Different Kind of Animal

Your gecko is nothing like a human or even a dog or a cat when it comes to behavior. But that's okay. It is this uniqueness that makes the gecko so special in our world.

Learn to appreciate your gecko's special ways by learning as much as you can about it and observing its behavior at every opportunity. Soon you will come to realize that geckos are quite wonderous creatures that should be appreciated for the unique critters that they are.

part four

Beyond
the ᐧ
Basics

chapter 9

Gecko Conservation

Everyone who has an interest in animals is aware that many species are having a hard time coping in our human-dominated world. As the human population continues to grow, we take more and more land for our own use. This often results in the displace-  ment of the native animals and plants that have lived on that land for millions of years.

Thousands of species of reptiles are among the many types of animals that are threatened the world over or have been completely eliminated due to habitat destruction, collection for the pet trade, and other human-related causes. Whether it be the building of condominiums on a parcel of land where a certain species breeds, or the ravages of war that wipe out every living thing in the war-torn area, human interference in the environment is taking its toll on reptiles.

119

A number of gecko species are among the reptiles that
are suffering from weakened populations as a result
of human action upon the land. While the majority of
gecko species are healthy and thriving in their environments despite the presence of humans, many species are in danger of extinction.

How Species Become Threatened

The two biggest problems for geckos in the wild are
habitat destruction and collection for the pet trade.
These are issues that affect geckos both abroad and in
the United States.

When a gecko's environment is graded, paved over,
and then built upon by humans, the geckos often have
nowhere to go. For gecko species that evolved to live
only in a very specific area, such as a remote island or
an isolated forest, this can be disastrous. As the gecko
population struggles to stay alive in its shrinking environment, the added stress of collection for the pet
trade can nearly wipe the species out.

Many species of gecko do not breed well in captivity.
Rather than eliminate these species from the pet trade,
some collectors will capture as many individuals as they
can to sell to reptile dealers, who will in turn sell them
to pet stores. In many cases, the native population of
geckos can't reproduce quickly enough to keep up
with the number of individuals that are taken from the
wild. Soon, the number of animals dwindles such that
they are threatened with extinction.

What is even more tragic about this scenario is that the
majority of collected geckos die after being captured.
Only a few individuals make it all the way to the pet
store alive, and then some perish once they are taken
home by those who purchase them.

Government Reponses

If you care about the health of the planet as well as
the diversity of reptile and gecko species in the
world, all this news about habitat destruction and the

decimation of species is very disturbing. You are not alone if you feel this way. All around the world, concerned individuals are joining together to help stop the ruination of the Earth's biodiversity.

In an effort to control the exploitation and destruction of reptiles and other exotic animals around the world, an international agreement was signed by more than 120 nations, including the United States, in the 1970s. This agreement, known as the Convention of the International Trade in Endangered Species (CITES), was designed to protect threatened species from poaching and international smuggling.

Under CITES, animals are grouped as follows: those in immediate danger of extinction; those not in immediate endanger of extinction but threatened and declining; and those that are rare but may be traded if the member nation deems it is appropriate. In all these classifications, the animals listed can only be traded under special permit. Permits are usually granted only to zoos and other facilities that plan to breed the animal in captivity and therefore further its continued existence rather than threaten it.

In the United States, animals that are in danger of dying out are protected under the Endangered Species Act, a federal law passed in 1973 that prohibits the distribution, collection, possession, or sale of certain endangered species; and the collection, captive breeding, and selling of other threatened species except by special permit.

Geckos in Peril

If you are a gecko fancier, brace yourself for bad news: Nearly fifty species of geckos are listed with CITES as threatened. All are Day Geckos from the Madagascar region, and their populations have been seriously depleted due to collection for the pet trade.

Among these threatened geckos are the Blue-Tailed Day Gecko, the Banded Day Gecko, and the Aldabra Day Gecko. These are not geckos you will typically see in pet stores or at herp shows but, because of their beauty and rarity, can command a large sum of money among collectors who obtain them through other means. Because of this, these species are all in danger of being wiped out.

The Gold Dust Day Gecko is one of the Day Geckos from Madagascar. Unfortunately, many related species are in serious decline.

The good news is that CITES is helping to slow down the destruction of these gecko species. Before CITES, no effective controls on the collection and trade of these species existed.

In the United States, only one species of gecko is on the Endangered Species List: the Monito Gecko. The Monito is a pale tan gecko around 36 millimeters in length, found only in a small section of Puerto Rico called Monito Island. Monito Island is a tiny piece of land covered with cacti, shrubs, and stunted trees growing from cracks in the limestone. The Monito gecko, which evolved on Monito Island and is isolated there, has no opportunity to expand its habitat.

In 1982, biologists surveyed the island and counted only 18 Monito Geckos. When the species was first discovered in 1974, scientists noticed that a large population of black rats had been introduced by humans to the island. They now believe that these predatory rats are the reason the Monito Gecko is struggling to survive.

What You Can Do

If you admire geckos or have an affinity for all animals, you can help stave off the destruction of geckos and other species on the planet.

GROUP ACTIVITIES

Join your local herpetological society. These societies often work to help protect reptiles by taking regular counts of local reptile populations. They also lobby legislators for laws that will protect reptile habitats, and they work to educate the public about the importance of saving reptiles in the wild.

Support conservation and ecology groups. Become active in protecting the environment by joining one or more organizations that work to save habitats and species from destruction. When you join these organizations, your membership dollars go toward lobbying legislators, educating the public, and even buying and protecting threatened land. Some examples of such groups are the Sierra Club, The Nature Conservancy, and the National Resources Defense Council.

WAYS TO HELP ON YOUR OWN

Don't take geckos or other animals from the wild. Even though a species may be plentiful, don't capture individual specimens from the wild to make them your pets. Every time you do this, you are compromising the species population just a little bit, and combined with other factors such as habitat and food source destruction, the species is weakened. Let wild animals stay wild.

Buy your geckos from pet shops or breeders, and purchase only those animals that have been captive-bred. Captive-bred geckos are healthier than those taken from the wild and are more likely to survive in a terrarium situation. In addition to supporting those breeding geckos in captivity, you will personally benefit from this action in the long run.

> ### A DELICATE BALANCE
>
> Every natural habitat develops so as to provide for all of its residents. For example, in a given environment, insects serve as food for reptiles and amphibians that in turn serve as food for birds. When a species is eliminated from the environment, or a species is introduced by humans, the natural balance of the habitat is disrupted. To do your part in maintaining the balance, leave wild animals in the wild, and do not release pet species into a wild environment.

Never release captive-bred geckos into the wild. Although you may feel that you are helping the wild population by adding more individuals to it, the reality is that captive-bred geckos can spread disease to wild geckos. Because they were born in captivity, geckos from your terrarium may harbor diseases or parasites to which they have become immune but that can eradicate a wild population that has no immunity to these organisms.

123

chapter 10

Recommended
Reading
and Resources

Magazines

Vivarium Magazine
American Federation of Herpetoculturists
P.O. Box 300067
Escondido, CA 92030-0067
(619) 747-4948

Reptile and Amphibian Magazine
1168 Route 61 Highway South
Pottsville, PA 17901

Reptiles Magazine
P.O. Box 6050
Mission Viejo, CA 92690

Books

Bartlett, R.D. and Bartlett, Patricia P. *Geckos.* Hauppauge, NY: Barron's
Educational Series, Inc. 1995.

McKeown, Sean and Zaworski, Jim. *General Care and Maintenance of Tokay Geckos and Related Species.* Lakeside, CA: Advanced Vivarium Systems, 1997.

de Vosjoli, Philippe. *The Lizard Keeper's Handbook.* Lakeside, CA: Advanced Vivarium Systems, 1997.

Veterinary Services for Reptiles

For information contact:

Wilber B. Armand, VMD
Box 605
Chester Heights, PA 19017
(610) 892-4812

Herpetoculturist Societies

Global Gecko Association
P.O. Box 739 Westview Station
Binghamton, NY 13905

American Federation of Herpetoculturists
P.O. Box 300067
Escondido, CA 92030-0067
(619) 747-4948

American Society of Ichthyologists and Herpetologists
Florida State Museum
University of Florida
Gainesville FL 32611

Maryland Herpetological Society
Department of Herpetology
Natural History Society of Maryland
2643 North Charles Street
Baltimore, MD 21218

The Minnesota Herpetological Society
c/o The Bell Museum of Natural History
10 Church Street SE
Minneapolis, MN 55455-0104

New England Herpetological Society
P.O . Box 1082
Boston, MA 02103

New York Herpetological Society
P.O. Box 1245
New York, NY 10163-1245

Northern California Herpetological Society
P.O. Box 1363
Davis, CA 95616

Philadelphia Herpetological Society
P.O. Box 52261
Philadelphia PA 19115-7261

The Pittsburgh Herpetological Society
c/o The Pittsburgh Zoo
One Hill Road
Pittsburgh, PA 15206

Rainforest Reptile Refuge Society
1395-176 Street
Surrey, British Columbia
Canada V4P 1M7

**Society for the Study of Amphibians
and Reptiles (SSAR)**
Karen Toepfer, Treasurer
P.O. Box 626
Hays, KS 67601-0626

South Texas Herpetological Society
P.O. Box 780073
San Antonio, TX 78278-0073

Southern California Herpetological Association
Michele A. Diller
P.O. Box 2932
Santa Fe Springs, CA 90670

Southern Nevada Herpetological Society
P.O. Box 4753
Las Vegas, NV 89127-0753

Southwestern Herp Society
P.O. Box 7469
Van Nuys, CA 91409

Volusia County Herpetological Society (Florida)
P.O. Box 250553
Holly Hill, FL 32125-0553